# Delicious Con

Reflections on autism, intimacy and communication

Phoebe Caldwell

# Delicious Conversations

Reflections on autism, intimacy and communication

© Phoebe Caldwell, 2012

The author has asserted their rights in accordance with the Copyright, Designs and Patents Act (1988) to be identified as the author of this work.

**Published by:**
Pavilion Publishing and Media Ltd
Rayford House
School Road
Brighton
BN3 5HX

**Tel:** 01273 43 49 43
**Fax:** 01273 73 22 08
**Email:** info@pavpub.com
**Web:** www.pavpub.com

Published 2012

All rights reserved. No part of this publication may be reproduced, stored in a retrieval system, or transmitted in any form or by any means, electronic, mechanical, photocopying, recording or otherwise, without prior permission in writing of the publisher and the copyright owners.

A catalogue record for this book is available from the British Library.

**ISBN:** 978-1-908993-05-2

Pavilion is the leading publisher and provider of professional development products and services for workers in the health, social care, education and community safety sectors. We believe that everyone has the right to fulfil their potential and we strive to supply products and services that help raise standards, promote best practices and support continuing professional development.

**Author:** Phoebe Caldwell
**Editor:** Kathleen Steeden, Pavilion
**Cover design:** Katherine Paine, Pavilion
**Page layout and typesetting:** Emma Garbutt, Pavilion
**Printing:** CMP Digital Print Solutions

# Limestone Country

*Fractured by frost, weathered by water's flow,*
*ground by the weight of glaciers long ago*
*that scratched out runnels, hollowed, bevelled, cleft,*
*the scars and scourings of its passing left;*
*this is a landscape whittled to the bone –*
*a sharp, smooth, flat and craggy land of stone.*

*But in the cracks, deep hidden, often missed*
*bloom secret gardens of the barren klist:*
*orchids and mountain avens, gentians blue,*
*delicate milkwort, cranesbill's burning hue.*
*Who in such bleached and arid waste would know*
*the sweetest flowers here in earth's wrinkles grow?*

Rosemary Russell

# Contents

**Chapter 1**
Introduction ..................................................................... 1

**Chapter 2**
Whose reality? ................................................................ 21

**Chapter 3**
Spaced out ..................................................................... 39

**Chapter 4**
Body language and conversation ........................................ 61

**Chapter 5**
Mimicry, copying, imitation and using body
language to communicate ................................................. 79

**Chapter 6**
Talking to myself ............................................................. 97

**Chapter 7**
A walk by the sea ........................................................... 111

**Chapter 8**
Compare and contrast ..................................................... 123

**Chapter 9**
'Happiest days of your life' .............................................. 141

**Chapter 10**
Behind the mirror ........................................................... 155

**Chapter 11**
Joined up islands ............................................................ 169

# About the author

**Phoebe Caldwell** started her career as a biologist. She is now an Intensive Interaction practitioner working mainly with children and adults on the autistic spectrum, many of whom have behavioural distress. Phoebe's methods combine using a person's body language to communicate, with paying attention to those aspects of an individual's environment that are triggering sensory distress. For four years Phoebe was a Rowntree Research Fellow looking at best practice. She teaches management, therapists, parents, teachers, advocates and carers, nationally and internationally, and she has been one of the principal speakers at a BILD annual conference. She is also employed by NHS, social services and community and education services to work with individuals they are finding it difficult to provide a service for. She has published seven books and four training films, and a number of academic papers. In 2010, she was awarded the Times/Sternberg Active Life Award for work on autism and contribution to the community, and in July 2011 Bristol University awarded her an Honorary Doctorate of Science for communication with people with autism.

# Chapter 1

# Introduction

## Autistic and neurotypical: what have we got in common?

This is a book about how we feel, particularly how we experience intimacy, in the form of a series of roving reflections. Set in the somewhat unlikely arena of autism – a condition that is characterised by aloneness, separation and inward focus – it is hardly the place where one might expect to start a journey to experience another mind.[1]

Instead of looking at people on the autistic spectrum as if they exist 'out there' on some strange other planet, I want to see what it is that we who are not autistic have in common with our autistic partners; to look at both of us from the point of view of whereabouts we are on the human spectrum, an inclusive attitude rather than one that sees us as separated. What do we share and what can we learn from what we are telling each other?

This train of thought is inspired by an email from a highly intelligent young man with Asperger's syndrome named Josh, who has no speech but communicates by typing either in English or in

---

1  Readers who are looking for more detailed information on the use of body language with people on the autistic spectrum will find examples in:
- Caldwell P & Horwood J (2008) *Using Intensive Interaction and Sensory Integration: A handbook for those who support people with severe autistic spectrum disorder*. London: Jessica Kingsley Publishers.
- Caldwell P (2005) *Finding You Finding Me*. London: Jessica Kingsley Publishers.
- Caldwell P & Horwood J (2007) *From Isolation to Intimacy: Making friends without words*. London: Jessica Kingsley Publishers.
- Caldwell P (2012) *Listening with All Our Senses*. Hove: Pavilion Publishing and Media Ltd.

Hebrew. Asked what it is like to experience Intensive Interaction, a way of communicating that uses body language rather than speech, (for example, does he feel it is humiliating or patronising?), his reply is that on the contrary, when his brain stops focusing it gives him the 'delicious feeling of having a conversation'.[2] What does Josh mean by this?

## Maintaining coherence

Autistic or not, we live in the same world; but it is evident that our interpretation of our sensory experience is different. Whereas those of us who are not autistic can, without difficulty, take in, process and put into context the images we see, the sounds we hear and the feelings we have, the brains of our autistic partners find it difficult to make sense of (and therefore interact with) incoming stimuli, both those that impact from outside the body and those that originate from inside. Sometimes the brain will function normally, placing sensory intake into context, and sometimes it will not. What Josh is telling us is that when he becomes stressed and the processing system in his brain is no longer effective (so his cognitive system is unavailable), if he is offered signals from a source outside himself, such as swinging the head (part of his behavioural repertoire), his brain recognises these easily. He can use this as a point of reference and so maintain some sense of being in touch. On the edge of losing reason this is an alternative channel for maintaining contact with the world outside himself. Rather than being an intrusion into his privacy or experienced as degrading, using Josh's body language to communicate with him offers him a lifeline.

So what is this delightful wordless connection that Josh can use when his cognitive faculties are under stress? How can we use this facility to explore how Josh feels and to recognise the feelings his choice of words engenders in us?

We immediately run into trouble, since talking about feelings can be immensely confusing. For example, autistic or not, there are some areas of experience where we all find that words are inadequate, particularly when it comes to expressing emotional

---

2   Harris J (2012) *Joshua's Planet* [online]. Available at: www.joshuasplanet.com (accessed June 2012).

state. We are going to have to start by thinking about what we mean in this context.

## Feeling as sensation, emotion or perception

In the search for appropriate language, confusion starts with the word 'feeling' itself, since we do not always distinguish between the three avenues of 'sensation', 'emotion' and 'perception' – fundamentally different processes haphazardly tossed into the same basket. On top of this, we do not always differentiate between one sensation and another. Take touch for example: because we use the same word for both senses, and because they have no specific and obvious organ such as an eye or an ear, it is easy to confuse the sensation of touch (our diffuse surface sensations) with the sensation of proprioception (the internal messaging system from our muscles and nerves that tells us what we are doing). In many cases they are interlinked and we register the superficial affect of a surface texture to the skin and the reactive pressure applied by our muscles and nerves simultaneously. For example, I fail to differentiate between the smooth sensation of a metal door knob and the exercise of my arm muscles as I open the door; I just don't think about them as separate feelings.

## Using body language to engage attention

Still at school, Martin is a happy young man of 17, that is, the world into which he has withdrawn does not distress him. He rocks and smiles and makes some attempts at speech, usually one syllable. He does not appear to like touch and will flinch if he is touched lightly but will occasionally rub his back and sides hard, and clearly enjoys it when I do likewise for him, applying firm pressure. However, Martin also has a puzzling behaviour: periodically he stretches his arms and hands right down to the ends of his fingers. This over-extension is so strong that the sinews stand out on the backs of his hands. This behaviour looks unnatural and does not appear to relate to whether he is happy or upset, it happens at any time. I am told it is not related to epilepsy. So how can I understand what is happening here?

I try it out on myself. At 6am I am starting to wake. I do not have to get up at once so I lie back in the half-light between night and morning, floating in penumbral dreams rather than being aware of my body. Time passes and the alarm rings. Before rising, I stretch – my toes upwards, ankles, calves, knees, thighs, chest, shoulders and particularly the joints of the spine – from my toes to the nape of my neck, bringing about sufficient body awareness to launch the transition from the horizontal to upright position. I need to know where I am, to get a clear picture of myself in relation to everything else, to feel my boundaries.

The question is: can this small exploration of my own behaviour cast any light on Martin's extensions? In my case, the sensations I have experienced suggest that my spread-eagled extension mobilises my musculature and helps me return to the daytime world as I define my physical boundaries. So is this what Martin (who appears to be low on proprioceptive stimuli), is periodically doing for himself? Is his apparently bizarre behaviour an adaptation to inadequate perception of proprioceptive stimulus, providing him with a sense of the boundaries of his self, defining his body limits so that he can, perhaps even unconsciously, perceive where he is and by implication what and who he is? Or is it a purely unconscious spasm related to a misfiring in the brain stem? If the latter is true, is it also helping him to know what he is doing when he reaches a state of confusion? Faced with alternatives such as these, we can only tell by responding to an individual's movements or sounds and seeing if this will spark their interest.

Making Martin's movements myself helps me to internalise and align myself with what he is getting out of the action (one that looks odd in my terms), in order to learn what his reality means to him, rather than looking at him from the outside and making judgments based on my own. But, in pursuit of an analogy I need to be careful. Just because my exploration of Martin's spasmodic stretching produces a physical sensation in me, it does not mean that it is necessarily correct for him. I have to be careful not to project my sensory responses onto Martin.

So is there any point in replicating an individual's actions? Will it lead me to a better understanding of their world and hence to the possibility of developing communication and engagement where there has been none? If I physically take on the rhythms of my conversation partner, will it help me to tune in to them? If so, what will this do for them?

From the point of view of engaging attention, it turns out that the exact trigger for a behaviour is less important than whether or not it is a familiar part of a partner's repertoire (and therefore has significance for their brain if we respond to it). Is this familiarity intriguing enough to re-orientate their focus from involuntary imprisonment in their inner world to engagement with the world outside themselves?

Janice is elderly and presents as being extremely anxious. She chews a towel repetitively and periodically wanders in an agitated manner. When she sits down on a sofa, I sit beside her and follow her jaw movements, exploring the feeling she is giving herself. Realising how rhythmic it is, I tap this rhythm on her knee. Her brain recognises this pattern and she comes out of her withdrawn state and starts to smile and take an interest in what I am doing. (I have shifted her attention from solitary self-stimulation to an activity we are sharing.) Her relaxation is palpable to all the staff present. She lies back and eventually doses off. Her support staff comment that they have not seen her so relaxed before.

So how is using touch to transmit a rhythm that Janice's brain recognises helping us to come into accord with each other?

According to the *New Oxford Dictionary of English*, our 'haptic sense' relates not only to our sense of touch, as in the perception and manipulation of objects using the senses of touch (superficial) but also as in proprioception (internal messages from the nerves and musculature about tension and pressure and movement).[3] Interwoven signals (a sort of global positioning network) help us to

---

3   *The New Oxford Dictionary of English* (1998) Oxford: Oxford University Press.

map our body and give us the sense of where we are in relation to 'other than our body' as well as its physical properties. The same duality applies to the other senses, such as vision.

> *'A special sense such as vision is processed at a special place within the body boundary, in this case the eyes. Signals from the outside are thus double. Something you see or hear excites the special sense of sight (or sound) as a non-body signal but it also excites a body signal hailing from the place in the skin where the special signal entered … When you see or hear, you do not just see or hear: you feel you are seeing something with your eyes or hearing it with your ears.'* [4]

It's not just information about the environment that is being gathered but also information about ourselves: 'what' and additionally 'that' we are, even if knowing about ourselves is not the primary point of focus. External stimuli not only tell us about the outside world but also inform us of our internal state; not just vis-à-vis ourselves but also in relation to the original stimulus. When I tap Janice's knee with a rhythm her brain recognises, it not only draws her attention to an outside source, but also sends her information about her own body. (I shall discuss the critical importance of confirmation later.)

So there is a third consequence to my observation. When I see, hear or feel an object or activity out there, it not only delivers information to me about it and about myself, but it also engenders in me a particular sensation (which may be positive or negative), one that carries its own particular affective charge – my response in relation to what I see, feel or hear. This feeling is specific. If I come across it again, or something like it, I shall revisit it. It and its allies are like provisions sorted, labelled and stored in a larder. If I turn my attention towards its 'flavour', I shall find that it will lift the lid on a whole group of metaphorical tastes stacked on the same shelf.

---

4   Damasio AR (1949) *Descartes' Error: Emotion reason and the human brain.* New York: GP Putnam's Sons.

As with touch, what we are looking at is 'feeling' as sensory perception, the emergence of 'cognitions' or 'inklings',[5] some so powerful that they carry us through into qualitative descriptions of emotion: 'I am very touched by this', or 'I'll be in touch'.

In practice, it is not just touch but all of my sensory experiences, both of the internal and the external world, that carry a definitive affective tag which can be recognised, isolated and revisited. Even the dull ones that may be experienced as boring are a sensory event, one that can be considered and acknowledged. Learning to identify a particular sensation provides me with an alternative navigational system to thinking, arguably a more primitive one, but one with the advantage of allowing access to my subterranean library. This is what Guy Claxton calls the 'undermind' – the stuff that is present in my brain but which I am not consciously aware of.[6] For me, the undermind feels as if it has the properties of a no man's land, somewhere I can send out occasional patrols at night when my conscious brain is quiet.

This affective process appears to connect with the undermind by means of a route that resembles resonance. Something that I am initially aware of externally sparks off related images in my undermind which tune in with the feeling that I derive from my original stimulant. In my case these 'once-removed' offspring will normally present as (fleeting) visual images, recognisable as related, but often tantalising in their transience, needing to be grabbed by the heels quickly before they scamper away. Less frequently, messengers deliver a half-heard auditory prompt: 'Try so and so…'.

There may be more than one of these images. If I see X in my conscious mind and X is associated with a certain feeling, my undermind will float up a number of 'x's, together with possible 'y's and 'z's, not necessarily identical but near enough to share at least some sensations with the original. Why bother with this exploration? What is wrong with just a description of X? What does Xx, Xy or Xz give me that I could not locate already by consciously

---

5   'Inklings' derives from the middle English verb to 'inkle', meaning 'to utter in an undertone', an ancestry that captures precisely the fleeting nature of these sensory messages (*The New Oxford Dictoionary of English* (1998) Oxford: Oxford University Press).
6   Claxton G (1997) *Hare Brain and Tortoise Mind: Why intelligence increases when you think less.* London: Fourth Estate.

bending my thoughts towards it, analysing it through logical progression? One answer seems to be that my awareness of an affective state (and consequent understanding) is expanded. I can tap back into a whole variety of alternative cognitions, which shed light on what may have been a previously intractable situation.

So far, black and white: either I know what I am doing or I feel what I am doing. When I think, I initiate and explore within the limits of my capacity – a conscious process that I feel I am in charge of. The affective process is a skinny dip into the undermind, which I allow to happen, in which I can float and swim in a medium that I am not immediately aware of.

It is this borderline area between 'conscious recollection' and the unconscious that is so intriguing. Are thinking and feeling really separate processes? If I cannot think without feeling, can I have a feeling without thinking?

Falling over an obstacle, my chest comes in contact with a heavy sharp object as it hits the ground and I crack a rib. Pain comes, urgent, followed by the almost but not quite contingent thought, 'My God, this hurts.' These are two separate apprehensions, the first fast-tracked through the amygdala, the second a cortical assessment of the degree of sensation.

Then there is 'brain-surfing', initial attention to a subject followed by emptying the mind, allowing affective connections to get to work, to resonate uncluttered by extraneous matter. We notice an as yet untamed flicker as an idea begins to crystallise but before we have words to express it. Characteristic of such ideas and associations is that they 'pop up' – in my case particularly when going to sleep or when waking and before I find words to frame them. Unless one can name these flickers quickly they vanish.

So are these affective thoughts just feelings unframed by words? And is feeling just the substrate for thought – there all the time, whether or not we pay attention to it? I find that during the process of crystallisation (cognitive actualisation) I can either frame the emerging idea in words, or snare it as feeling in metaphor, a vivid picture as yet not formulated in words. Of course, thought and perception are intricately interwoven and I am constantly using both, crossing and recrossing the boundaries, testing one intuition against the other, checking which of these enticements is relevant and which is not. At least I now have a choice, I am not stuck with the so-called obvious (which can be very misleading).

In order to effect transfer from one layer into the other there are conditions to be met. The first is that an underlying affective match already exists. Have I already met this feeling, or a near-enough match to be recognised as closely related to it? Second, the interface needs to be clear of irrelevant material so that my insight can surface. Finally, I need to be aware that my insight, illuminating as it may appear to me, may be wrong.

As I write this I am aware that while the brain's overall goal of self-actualisation is the same in all of us, the exact point at which any of us lie on the spectrum of affective/thinking differs. I am probably at the extreme end of the affective scale, which works out in practice as a dizzying ride from one perception to another, leapfrogging logic through resonant metaphor, risky but occasionally proving inspirational. I recognise (and sometimes envy) rational processing in others and have had to learn to complement my free-wheeling excursions with analysis. A and B may share the same resonant sensation (qualia) but what is the link and is it really applicable in this instance? What light, if any, does such a 'hop, skip and jump, procedure throw on this present circumstance?

In her excellent and revealing film *Jam Jar*, Donna Williams (who has severe autism) tells us about yet another way that she engaged in her search to make sense of her environment: 'People say there's only one way of thinking but I think there's all sorts of different ways of thinking.'[7] She goes on to tell us that, due to problems with processing speech, she could not always make sounds into words and the words into meaning and put the meaning in context, since they all required interpretation. So she developed what she calls the 'system of sensing', building up a sensory encyclopaedia of sensations for different objects, For example, the table was a 'brown, flat, square, thud thing'. Using such an approach she was able to maintain some sort of connection with her surroundings.

7    Williams D (1995) *Jam Jar*. Film. Fresh Film in association with Channel 4, UK.

Nevertheless, in a world that, in her words, demanded that she lived through interpretation, the struggle to do so was extremely stressful and created a war in her head from which it was easier to retreat into her inner world.

While one might object that such a system of sensing excludes the possibility of generalisation, Donna tells us that she managed without interpretation, it was redundant to her. (In this context it is interesting that even partners with extreme autism can manage to generalise if such a generalisation takes place in the context of, what is for them, meaningful sensory experience and not in the realm of cognitive interpretation. 'I know that you will answer me if I flick my string, how about if I bang the sink?' It would seem that the process of generalisation itself is not the problem so much as the mode in which it is being organised and expressed.)

In this inner world of autism, the brain is able to focus by concentrating on a single (or limited number) of physical sensations that become hardwired in through endless repetition, becoming so familiar that they succeed in bypassing the processing system. What the observer witnesses is a repetitive behaviour that reflects a conversation between the brain and body which is intelligible to their autistic partner and helps them to avoid sensory overload and stress, to 'hang on in'. The brain sends messages to the body that tells it to initiate a sound or movement. This sends feedback to the brain which it recognises, an input that in the swirling chaos provides a point of reference and allows it to stay on track. Now at least there is something in the person's environment that makes sense and helps them maintain coherence. Tito Rajarshi Mukhopadhyay speaks about how the reflections of shadows and flapping his hands by a mirror made him feel secure. He knew what to expect from them.[8] Understanding the world through physical sensation is quite a different process from analysis through cognition – or through the matching resonance of affective and intuitive twinges.

Donna Williams' work illuminates not only the world of autism but also our own processes and the way that we struggle with what we have. Recent research suggests that the brain may even have its

[8] Mukhopadhyay TR (2008) *How Can I Talk if My Lips Don't Move? Inside my autistic mind.* New York: Arcade Publishing.

own refuse collection system in the form of daydreaming (which is distinct from dreaming in sleep). Far from being an idle process to be actively discouraged ('Stop daydreaming child and attend!'), this mode of brain activity is a default mechanism which it reverts to when not actually engaged in thinking. It can be envisaged as a kind of auditing, 'where the default network, a cluster of regions arching through the midline of the brain from back to front', talks to the hippocampus (the memory store), selecting those memories that are important enough to catalogue and store, and discarding the rest so that the brain does not become overloaded. So important is this apparent resting process that when the brain is engaged in this way it uses far more energy than when it is in thinking mode – and even more than the beating heart.[9] There is also evidence of this tidying activity during early sleep.

In direct contrast to daydreaming (low on attention but high on metabolic requirement), meditation is highly focused and low on energy demands. Laying aside whether its primary intention is spiritual or secular, the world stills for the person practising. One of the side-effects of meditation is that attention to emptying the mind of its business unblocks the channels of process. The interface between the conscious and undermind becomes more and more porous: buried but resonant material is more easily accessed, identified, compared and expanded. For me, the tree of possibilities flowers and my practice is enriched.

Still prowling around in the maze of 'feeling', we come to emotion, a term which, as Damasio points out, is frequently restricted to self-orientated concern.[10] What is clear is that we often find it difficult to handle the surges of passion that are part of our makeup.

Steering clear of purple prose, words mutate, changing nuance if not absolute meaning. Nowadays 'emotional' is a term that carries a whole baggage of projection: oceans of teddy bears and flowers wrapped in plastic. In his fascinating book on the Japanese concept of *Wabi-Sabi*, a metaphysical attitude that draws attention to the states of imperfection and transience, Leonard Koren suggests that

---

[9] Raichle M, MacLeod AM, Snyder AZ, Powers WJ, Gusnard DA & Shulman G (2001) A default mode of brain functioning. *Proceedings of the National Academy of Sciences of the United States of America* **98** 676–682.

[10] Damasio AR (2000) *The Feeling of What Happens*. London: William Heinemann, p56.

we are losing direct contact with how we feel. He writes that the expression of our passions:

> '*is being progressively ironed out in an accelerating trend towards the uniform digitilisation of all sensory experience, wherein an electronic "reader" stands between experience and observation, and all manifestation is encoded identically*'.[11]

We are in danger of losing our capacity to bare our feelings.

Losing touch with our own feelings, we vicariously hunt down and share the desolation of strangers. When a microphone is thrust in their face, victims and their neighbours say, 'It feels very emotional' and we are caught up in the second-hand flow of their desolation, but without the responsibility that comes from owning it. So I will mainly use the term, 'affect' rather than 'emotion' to express how we feel.

## Second-person engagement

A side-effect of our withdrawal is that some people, even professionals, find affect so difficult to handle in their own lives that they feel uncomfortable with any discussion of feeling, excluding it from permissible interaction. Allied to this is the problem of how to encode affect, no matter how moving the interaction appears. So the practitioner may feel manoeuvred into evaluating joy by getting out their ruler to measure proximity.

This is clearly absurd and leads to the suspicion that in our desire for scientific detachment we have been led into an intellectual cul-de-sac, in particular we are confusing the cerebral and affective processes – how we think with how we feel. In her groundbreaking book *How Infants Know Minds*, Vasu Reddy distinguishes three different ways of engaging with other minds. The first-person approach knows other minds as an extension of self. The third-person approach is detached, and views them through observation. The core of her book

---

[11] Koren L (1994) *Wabi-Sabi for Artists, Designers, Poets and Philosophers.* Berkeley, CA: Stone Bridge Press.

is an alternative, the second-person response approach, 'where others are experienced as others in direct emotional engagement'. She points towards the difference between being the subject of a smile from a friend and observing a smile directed at another person: in the former case, being its subject is experienced as 'phenomenally different' and calls for an affective response.[12]

# Should practitioners engage with feelings?

Working towards establishing communication with people who have little or no speech, the question is still occasionally raised as to whether or not it is part of my role as practitioner to engage with affect. However obliquely, one school of thought suggests that such work should be confined to analyses of what we see happening, rather than trying to understand our partner's feelings. The implication is that involvement with (and interpretation of) affect is unscientific. But this suggestion raises the whole question of the role of the practitioner. Is it legitimate for them to align with and interpret their therapeutic partner's feelings or should they confine themselves to observation and recording data? Critically, in order to improve our understanding, how can I pin down something as nebulous as my assessment of my partner's feeling, define it accurately and pass it on to you, so that you receive an accurate evaluation of our affective interaction? To put it another way: how can I help you to taste its flavour?

# Do people with autism have feelings?

Because we find it difficult to read the body language and hence the affective state of those on the autistic spectrum, (since it does not necessarily correspond with ours), it is often assumed that they do not feel emotions. Therese Jolliffe, who has severe autism, warns us that it is not true to suggest that people with autism lack

---

12   Reddy V (2008) *How Infants Know Minds*. Cambridge, MA: Harvard University Press.

feelings. She says: 'We do love people and feel lonely',[13] but they have problems with the feedback they get from their bodies. Temple Grandin describes emotion as being totally overwhelming, 'like a tidal wave'.[14] In the introduction to his book, *Look Me in the Eye: My life with Asperger's*, John Elder Robison (who is on the Asperger's end of the autistic spectrum) writes: 'Above all, I hope this book demonstrates once and for all that however robotic we Aspergians might seem, we do have deep emotions.'[15]

# The difficulties inherent in transmission of feeling

So what can I hope to know about my partner's affective state? And do my speculations add to our understanding? In a personal sense, just as it is difficult for you to know what I mean when I do not make it exactly clear in what sense I am using the term 'feeling', so it can also be extremely hard to find language that accurately transmits to you what it is that I am actually feeling, and to be sure we are talking about the same thing. One person's feeling may be another's black hole. On the other hand, in talking about valuing the quiddity (essence) of another human being, what we now intuit about communication suggests that it is not enough to observe and record the actions of our partners without also considering how they feel. An autistic man tells us that he likes it when people tune into him.[16] So while it may not be possible for us to record affective relationship 'uncontaminated' by our own responses, just because it is difficult it does not mean that it is not worth trying.

Even if we do decide that it is legitimate to be working with our partner's feelings, they are not easy to describe and pass on to a third party in such a way that transmits the same meaning for both of us or that offers us an absolute standard. As we search for acceptable language we have to bear in mind that the sensory experience of people with autism is completely different to ours and that we shall be led badly astray if we assume it is the same.

13   Jolliffe T, Lansdown R & Robinson C (1992) Autism: a personal account. *Communication* **26** (3) 12–19.
14   *A is for Autism* (1992) Film. Fine Take Productions with Channel 4.
15   Robison JE (2008) *Look Me in the Eye: My life with Asperger's*. New York: Ebury Press.
16   O'Brian A (undated) Personal communication wiuth the author.

# Using metaphor to transmit the essence of a feeling

Sometimes the only way to capture the essence of sensory experience is to engage with an image that has common resonance for both of us, through the language of simile and metaphor. If what my partner feels sparks off an image in me, it may also resonate for you. Trained as a scientist, I am well aware of the danger that coming at a subject through such a subjective approach lays it open to the use of figurative and emotive language. But in snatching a passing metaphor, can I hitch a ride on it and see how far it will take me? Can I cadge a lift home; bring it to internal presence so that I see the feeling from inside and from here can convey it to you?

If it is powerful enough, a relevant image will transform a description into a sensation. A striking example is offered to us by an able child on the autistic spectrum. His general progress at school is good but he is struggling with French. He tells his mother that he has problems with this particular classroom: 'It's like being in a car-compactor.' This eloquent description of the sensory difficulties he experiences (a claustrophobic sensation of life-threatening pressure due to the phenomenon of lack of permanence, whereby dimensions can expand or shrink without warning) hits the affective target squarely – bulls eye. Instead of struggling with details, I now know what this feels like. The image the child offers of the sensation he has experienced literally triggers a sensory response; it 'feels in me'.

Despite the idea that people with autism lack the ability to think flexibly, they can be extremely good at giving us insights into the sensations they experience. Like the child who tells me that light touch feels like 'a whole load of spiders trying to crawl out of my skin'. All of her skin sensors are firing at once. Looking at the powerful feeling this initiates in me, I suspect the picture presented is so vivid that it is activating a sensory motor pattern in my brain – just as I experience a slight shiver when offered the more familiar description of 'a goose walking over my grave', as the cold 'slap-slap' of webbed feet imprints the marrow of my bones.

Metaphors offer a two-way process in the development of understanding. I align myself with the empathetic images of others, tuning myself in to their experience, able to resonate with their perceptions. I offer you my sensory experience in a package that I hope will give you an internal model, one that strikes a chord in you. This is the way we learn about each other, not just as objects that can be assessed but as living realities to whom we can relate. The hope is that this exploratory approach may lead us to open up new perspectives.

## Accounts from people on the spectrum

The question that still needs to be answered is whether, in this sensitive territory of relationship, an attitude of intuitive (and sometimes imaginative) process can take us any further in the shared journey with our partner (as subject), than that of an expert who has an agenda to impart to their student (as a 'sometimes-unable-to-co-operate' object).

Is it legitimate to place my feelings alongside the supposed feelings of my partner, and what are the limitations of reading personal experience into body language? How can we build in checks to circumscribe any wilder flights of fancy? In order to be of value, we need to harness multiple sources for any discussion on the affective state of our partners, testing one against the other. Together, do they build a coherent picture?

First, we now have the considerable literature placed at our disposal by people with autism themselves in the form of memoirs, film, video and audiotape. Particularly useful is the Channel 4 film *Jam Jar* where, among other insights, Donna Williams discusses how she processes her sensory intake.[17] Accounts from Gunilla Gerland, Therese Jolliffe, Temple Grandin, Lindsey Weekes, Kamran Nazeer, John Elder Robison (a brilliant man with Asperger's syndrome), and the remarkable Tito Rajarshi Mukhopadhyay with his poems and stories, can help us to understand how it feels to experience autism.

---

17   Williams D (1995) *Jam Jar*. Film. Fresh Film in association with Channel 4, UK..

Second, there are conversations with autistic people themselves. 'Listening' to what Joshua Harris tells us on his website, we can understand that when his brain processing system is becoming confused, using his body language to get in touch with him (Intensive Interaction) 'feels like having a delicious conversation'.[18] In a world where his sensory distress is triggering his body's self-defence system, it helps him to maintain coherence. At the other end of the emotive scale is an unnamed man, fixated on leaves, distraught because the mower has run through a pile of them and cut them up. His coherence is destroyed and he exclaims: 'They are killing my friends, they are killing all my friends.' It is not necessary to be deeply intuitive to sense the feelings that prompt observations such as these, running through the complete spectrum of affect, from delight to desolation.

Third, there are quite a surprising number of people on the autistic spectrum who, if one listens to the way they speak, are apparently splitting their personalities into 'good' person and 'bad' person, an unconscious strategy that is explored in Chapter 10. In this case our partner's feelings are expressed through completely differently sounding voices – one cheerful and the other (sometimes) savage – as they struggle to come to terms with the negative responses they have received and the images they have of themselves. Socially acceptable attitudes grapple with suppressed feelings. Acknowledge the darkness, either verbally or through body language, and we meet a third voice, centred and breathing relief. Someone has understood how they really feel. Since our sense of who we are is largely derived from our sensory picture of ourselves, confirmation of our partner's negative self gives them permission to be who they really feel they are, a position from which they are normally divorced since they are barred from feeling and expressing their 'bad bits'.

# Reading our partner's behaviour

So far we have been concerned with the expressions of people who have speech. What about those who do not?

---

[18] Harris J (2012) *Joshua's Planet* [online]. Available at: www.joshuasplanet.com (accessed June 2012).

Chapter 1: Introduction

Intensive Interaction is an approach to communication that focuses on the body language our partner displays. In one of many discussions we have had about the use of body language to interact, Michelle O'Neill suggested:

> *'I also think of it as affective attunement, listening to the quality of my partner's body language so that I can respond to how they feel.'* [19]

Those who care daily for non-verbal people with autism are usually quite good at judging whether they are having a 'good day' or a 'bad day'. This is a skill that depends on reading body language, how people are making their movements and sounds, and one which improves as we learn that people's body language is the voice of their affect. But 'good' or 'bad' days represent gross affect, amounting to an expression of mood rather than a response to the brain's running commentary on events as they happen, any small incident of which may register as threat. In people with autism, where the autonomic nervous system is on red alert, the threshold for setting off the body's self-defence system is at floor level.[20] Maybe I smile at you. If you are experiencing emotional overload, instead of getting a nice warm feeling – 'this woman likes me' – your body may implode under pressure from the tidal wave of sensation that is the autonomic storm in all its sensory violence. So by way of counterchecks and constraints, working with people whose behaviour is often labelled as severely challenging and whose stress levels are extremely high, if my interpretation is faulty, my partner will run away or I shall get thumped. Both responses leave little room for doubt as to how my partner feels.

For example, I have been asked by a consultant psychiatrist to see if I can find ways of engaging the attention of a young man with severe autism who is living at home. His behaviour is so disturbed that it is no longer possible to find people who are willing to work with him. Using his sounds and movements, we are able to communicate and are getting along fine; he is smiling and eager to engage. I allow myself to be lulled by his contentment into responding and moving into one of his initiatives, touching his hand when he is not looking.

---

19  O'Neill M (date unknown) Personal communication with the author.
20  The autonomic nervous system regulates systems that are not under conscious control, for example, breathing, heartbeat, sweating and the digestive system.

He immediately lashes out. In my enthusiasm for our interaction, I have overlooked the fact that his brain cannot manage stimuli that are unexpected. (If he loses touch with what is happening it triggers his self-defence system. He feels as though he is being attacked and responds accordingly.) I have let my feeling of pleasure at our engagement override his urgent need to know what is happening. Lesson learned. We can now proceed on the basis of his sensory experience rather than mine.[21]

If our partner is disturbed, we may not have time to sit back and think. Danger sharpens the wits and under these circumstances intuition and analysis need to be contingent. Go with the flow but watch your navigational instruments. Fortunately, this complex sounding process is not nearly as difficult as it sounds, since it appears that our brains are equipped to do it naturally.

---

21  Caldwell P (2006) *Finding You Finding Me*. London: Jessica Kingsley Publishers.

# Chapter 2

# Whose reality?

## The egocentric world

All of us live in an egocentric world based on the assumption that the reality that other people see, feel and hear is the same as that which we experience ourselves. We share a common sensory world – my world, and if yours is different from mine then I am right and you are wrong. I know this to be true because my senses tell me that it is so.

Unfortunately, this restricted vision limits my capacity to share experience with others, particularly when it leads me to make judgments about their behaviour and base my strategies on such blinkered assessments. It is one thing to know that there are alternatives but quite another to internalise such understanding and make it the basis of a relationship rather than an obstacle to be avoided. Even if we can stretch our imaginations far enough to take this different point of view on board, the effort of remembering to hold it in place and to make it the mainspring of our behaviour often appears to be more than we can manage.

This is a problem that occurs frequently when we are supporting people whose behaviour may appear to us to be isolating, bizarre or sometimes personally threatening. What are they hiding from? Why do they feel they need to hit or bite us? Instinctively we try to stop them, to manage them into line with our reality where we feel more comfortable with them, more likely to be able to control them.

In response to the query of what can be done in the situation where a young man is trying to strip the T-shirt from a female member of his support staff, I ask what colour it is (black with white stripes) and if he does it when she is wearing a plain shirt (no). Far from being a sexually motivated attack, the problem here is that this particular pattern throws an intolerable burden on his visual processing system, one that can be very painful and trigger the body's self-defence system. His sensory experience is of acute pain, leading to a self-protective behaviour – one that we, in the light of our own experience, interpret as deviant. It is so easy to mistake motives and to look for solutions in the wrong place when we see things differently.

# Flexing our imaginations: alternative versions of reality

In this chapter I want to look at alternative versions of the world we share – and it is easiest to do this in the company of artists. First we need some practice in flexing our neurotypical (non-autistic) imaginations. To do this we shall play a game that helps us to see things through the eyes of others.

Imagine that we are standing on the steps of the National Gallery in London's Trafalgar Square. Nelson's Column stands erect and beyond, Palladian facades recede into the distance, a perspective that comes to rest in the Palace of Westminster. Look at this prospect newly minted through the eyes of Canaletto. This picture is an architectonic perspective: cornices, pediments, porticos, windows, columns and architraves, every symmetrical detail lovingly portrayed. People in bright coloured clothes cluster in small lively groups, actively engaged with each other and in occupations. The scene seethes with business.

Now swap over to the same vista as it might appear in a picture by L S Lowry. Nelson's column is an etiolated factory chimney puffing grey smoke. In the same broad street, the faces of the buildings are blank and the people in the crowds are on the whole, separate – even when close to each other, they appear to be wrapped to their own thoughts, bent and scurrying out of the picture – grim times.

Finally, we look at the same scene as it might be seen through the eyes of Salvador Dali. Icons melt. The people have gone, the column wilts and the Victor of the Nile hangs upside down like a dying tulip over empty flower beds. A lion sits somewhere in the corner scratching his flank. Big Ben melts to a surreal puddle near the steps of the Cenotaph.

Energetic, tired and weird: this is the same prospect seen through different perspectives, in the sense that each incorporates the eye of the beholder. One might object that these three different flights of our fancy represent just this, how the artists see or how they want us to see. However, while their treatment of their material may be culturally specific and historically embedded, it does give those of us who are observers the possibility of alternative realities, viewpoints that are not our own.

As important as different aspects of the reality we share is that these glimpses give us access to how the artist feels about what they see. Even if their style is a matter of conscious choice, one can step back and ask what it is that led the artist to make this choice – the subject and style being only a kick-off point for the affective game that is subsequently played out.

# Artists on the spectrum

There are some artists whose drawings and paintings reveal not just their idiosyncratic and personal take on life, but also a much closer look at how they actually take in and process the world that we share. Whether or not they are on the autistic spectrum, they open a window that allows us to look in and ask what it is about their work that draws us into a closer understanding of the intricacies of their sensory perception. What is different about it?

The first is the art savant, Stephen Wiltshire. We are left open-mouthed at his astonishing panoramas of cities, drawn from memory after the briefest of glances. Unlike the rest of us his brain does not filter out what it deems to be unimportant. This capacity to see and hold everything is characteristic of some people on the autistic spectrum, although their intake is not normally accompanied by total retention – more often it drowns in the details of sensory confusion and in the worst cases, a morass of swirling pixels.

Donna Williams tells us that she sees all the detail but not the whole.[22] Ros Blackburn expresses the same condition slightly differently: she sees details but cannot put them into context.[23] What is different about Stephen (who has Asperger's syndrome) is that he not only encompasses the detail of what he sees but he also retains it. His brain seems to behave like a Polaroid camera, instantly recording and developing scenes in incredible clarity. He has no need to revisit his subject.

The next two painters are Joash Woodrow and Vilhelm Hammershoi. Woodrow was almost certainly on the Asperger's end of the autistic spectrum. His early paintings are primitive, almost childlike, secretive houses lurking behind trees. Sometimes a solitary figure peers out of the single window. His later pictures are astonishing, at times almost frenzied as though he is attacking the canvas or board, or any old bit of sacking he had picked up from a gutter. The texture is often rough since he uses any medium he has to hand such as whitewash or bitumen. He paints the same subjects again and again: landscapes that carry echoes of Eastern Europe, houses half hidden by rows and rows of whitewashed palings.

To see Woodrow's work for the first time is to experience the violence of his fixation. He lived in solitude and never exhibited. When he died his house was found to contain 700 pictures, for which galleries and public buildings are now competing. It is great art.

Hammershoi is Danish. Although he worked in Britain, his work is not well known outside his own country. According to a documentary introducing his paintings, he lived in the latter half of the 19th century and died in 1916.[24] Like Woodrow he was a retiring man but unlike him his paintings are subdued, with a restricted palette of dirty white through cream to brown and black. Most are of interiors although there are some paintings of

---

22   Williams D (1993) *My Experience with Autism, Emotion and Behaviour*. Documentary aired on *Eye to Eye with Connie Chung*. CBS.
23   Blackburn R (2002) Flint NAS seminar. 16 July 2002.
24   *Michael Palin and the Mystery of Hammershoi* (2008) Television programme. London: BBC Four. 29 June 2008.

buildings. The interesting thing about the latter is that they were always seen from an unusual prospect, rooftop or sideways on. He avoids face-on views. For example, where the subject is the British Museum, Hammershoi does not portray its splendid portico but rather paints a discreet view from the west side, the picture itself being dominated by meticulous and perseverant cast-iron railings marching away towards Gower Street in the distance. Many of his interiors (he painted more than 60 of them) are of empty rooms in his house. Where figures are present, they are half hidden or posed with back turned to the observer, the only highlight being the back of the neck. In one particularly interesting painting Vilhelm's wife Ida appears in the original, but subsequently the portion containing her figure has been folded out of sight round the back of the frame. Where there are no figures, what makes these pictures so compelling (one might almost call them portraits of rooms), is the lambent light, diffuse and soft at the edges so that in spite of half-opened doors and windows, it appears to be self-generating. As Michael Palin points out, these are mysterious paintings. What we are offered is the feeling of the room, an orchestration of affect rather than (or perhaps in spite of) representations of its walls and furniture: a quiet inducement to walk in but tread softly, invitations to 'this is how they feel to the artist', his authentic experience.

There are certain indications in Hammershoi's work that suggest the mystery mentioned in connection with his name may possibly be ascribed to his being on the (at the time unrecognised) autistic spectrum. These features are rather isolated but looked at together they add up to a man who was personally shy, lacking in self-confidence and living in a world where he preferred to avoid people. He took a peripheral view even of objects, avoided confrontation and eye contact, and in his mature works used a very withdrawn and restricted palette. He was prone to repetition in his choice of subject and fascinated in his landscapes by the perseverant and orderly retreat of railings into the distance – like Woodrow and his palings. Whether it is legitimate to push this a little further, when he does introduce figures he seems to be fascinated by the back of the neck, which is often the only part of the picture on which light falls. One of the features of autism is that the onset of sensations of disorder, chaos and pain are sometimes described as starting with a 'fizzy' feeling in the nape of the neck. People on the spectrum whose brain is overloading will often slap themselves in this specific region. It is an area of bodily importance to those with autism, particularly those who are disturbed.

Finally, there is the anonymous child in the film *A is for Autism*.[25] At school this little boy is already a gifted draftsman. His representations of train engines, tracks and signals, and all the paraphernalia of railways are extremely accurate. Looking back, he describes his first drawing. The subject is streetlights. One might expect to see a vertical line with a blob on top but instead he presents us with wriggly lines jerking all over the page. Such is his subsequent attention to detail it becomes clear that this does not represent a mistake, this is what he saw. What the neurotypical eye perceives as a straight vertical is jumping about for him. His visual perception is different from ours. He deals with this by fixating on railway lines and by extension engines, and contrasts these with roads: 'They go nowhere and end up at a level crossing.' Railways have destinations, they are finite, unlike roads which wander in all directions. By this strategy the boy literally gets back on track.

Like the imaginary visual game of artists in Trafalgar Square, these artists on the autistic spectrum (or at least on its periphery) – Wiltshire, Woodrow, Hammershoi and the unnamed child – give us access to versions of realities other than our own. The issue here is not so much their affective vision but rather that the style of their painting gives us a clue as to how their brains are processing what they see.

The effect that it has on us is to shift us from our own inner cartography into the perceptive world of someone else. Listening with the heart we see and learn to accept different versions of the world we share. If we are going to gain any understanding of what it is like to be on the autistic spectrum, we are going to have to be prepared to make a radical shift from our own sensory perspective.

# The autistic reality

Autistic or not, we spend our lives trying to make sense of the world around us and the people we encounter. We interpret our sensory

---

25  *A is for Autism* (1992) Film. Directed by Tim Webb. Fine Take Productions with Channel 4.

intake in such a way that it has significance and context for us. Page by page we write and rewrite the story of our lives. But to live with autism is to live with a damaged filtration system. Sometimes the brain can capture and make sense of images or words, sometimes these are just glimpses, or noises with no meaning at all. At other times the sounds are totally distorted, they boom or even slip right away. It is difficult for the person to curate these sensory inputs and form any coherent picture of what is going on. When their senses do return they may have no sense of attachment to what has been happening around them.

# Overloading

For people on the spectrum, while their organs of perception – their eyes, ears and skin – may be operating in the same range as the rest of us, by the time their brain has finished with the incoming messages, their sensory experience is of a reality quite different to that which those of us outside the autistic experience see, feel and hear. Their brain is failing to process all the stimuli that present themselves. The 'sorting office' is overwhelmed and becomes swamped with unprocessed images, sounds and sensations, an effect that is particularly well illustrated in Donna Williams' film *Jam Jar* where she shows us the sensory effect of shopping in a supermarket. As she passes the potato crisp shelves, she comments on the packet colours and how she can take on board the red ones and the blue, but by the time she has looked at the purple and green her processing system is bottlenecked: surplus images start to stack up, floating around in her brain. Adding to her visual overcrowding are all of the people moving around with trolleys and 'the noises of the tills pinging and fridges and lights humming. It's all happening too fast'.[26] The sensory information that we who are not autistic take in and process without thinking about it, has for Williams become a swirling mass of undigested inputs, a kaleidoscope in which the patterns never come to rest.

---

26  Williams D (1995) *Jam Jar*. Film. Fresh Film in association with Channel 4, UK.

## Coping strategies

This is just a beginning. Faced with a tidal wave of unprocessed stimuli, and in an effort to bring order to a chaotic situation, what happens next depends on exactly how the brain chooses to defend itself against the onslaught; it has various coping strategies. The most universal is a desperate attempt by the brain to maintain coherence by burying itself in a repetitive behaviour. By homing in on a particular sensation the brain hopes to exclude surplus stimuli and control the rising panic. When our conversation partners do focus on this particular activity, they know what they are doing. Alternatively, the brain can take steps to escape the situation that is overloading it by hiding in one way or another: covering the eyes, pulling a blanket over the head, sticking fingers in the ears or running away. Other alternatives are to freeze, switching off the cognitive faculties (sometimes completely), or to attack the person who, rightly or wrongly, they perceive as being the source of the overload. Some people may turn their aggression against themselves.

So what does it feel like to be a foot soldier fighting through this sensory battleground? And how can I get some sense of the consequent need to bury oneself in a physical sensation?

## Focusing on physical sensations

One day I am stuck in a hotel lift of unusual construction, a dumb waiter adapted for wheelchairs, delivering guests rather than meals – but delivering neither when the landing doors fail to open. There seems to be no alarm button so I have to resort to beating the panels with my fists. Outside I can hear people come and go but their voices rise from below in muffled waves, a series of dull booms that do not enlighten me as to what they are doing. I have no way of knowing what is happening. I am on a rising platform, open to the shaft and with no ceiling; my fertile imagination gets to work as to whether or not I run the risk of being squashed if the lift restarts and rises to the top. I am cut off. As time passes, in order to stem the incoming tide of panic I find myself gripping the steel rail, focusing on its cold steel shiny surface and on the physical feedback that my palms draw from its sensory qualities. All that I have now to maintain coherence is touch, a deep sense of proprioception as I press ever harder, and vision. Communication has let me down. Scary, especially when the lights go out.

I am in a situation that my self-defence system tells me is dangerous, at least potentially. I am afraid. And when I feel in danger of being overwhelmed by fear I take refuge, focusing my attention on a tactile/proprioceptive stimulus to control my stress reaction.

Describing this to a colleague, she pointed out that this must be what it is like to be autistic when the brain becomes overloaded and there is no longer any link between 'in here' and 'out there'. I have had the experience of not knowing what is going on and the feeling of drowning in incoherence and threat, desperately seeking coherence from a physical contact that still makes sense to me.

Internalisation is an affective rather than an analytic process. Now that I have been put through this helter-skelter of sensations I can empathise more easily with Therese Jolliffe when she tells us that she spends her whole life in terror, trying to work out the pattern of what is happening.[27] My limited ordeal lasts about half an hour and my recovery is speeded by a large glass of whisky brought to my room to 'steady the [rampaging] nerves'. There is no such escape for those on the 24/7 dislocation that characterises autism. The nightmare endures night and day.

There is a remarkable consistency in the descriptions by people on the autistic spectrum of their determined and sometimes frantic attempts to cling on to reality when the brain is 'losing it' and beginning to go into 'fragmentation', also called the 'autonomic maelstrom'.[28] Temple Grandin informs us that her brain is in a constant state of over-arousal. On the edge of chaos, all appear to seek stabilisation in physical feedback. Donna Williams describes how she 'desperately searched the eyes in the mirror, looking for

---

27  Jolliffe T, Lansdown R & Robinson C (1992) Autism: a personal account. Communication 26 (3) 12–19.

28  The autonomic nervous system is the part of our nervous system that organises the bodily systems that are not consciously under our control, such as sweating, heart rate, digestion etc. The term, 'autonomic maelstrom', coined by Ramachandran, conjures up for us a picture of the autonomic nervous system on the rampage, instigating messages that tell our partner's brain that they are in mortal danger (Ramachandran VS (2011) *The Tell-tale Brain*. Berkeley, CA: Harvard University Press).

something that had meaning, something to hold on to'.[29] Gunilla Gerland describes how, when she heard the sound of a motorbike revving and lost her sense of up and down, she gripped a fence very hard so that she could focus on the physical sensation she derived from the pressure.[30] In Kamran Nazeer's book *Send in the Idiots*, Andre finds that if it is too noisy in a busy pub he can maintain coherence by spilling a small quantity of beer on the bar top and doodling in it.[31]

My panicky adventure in the lift seems minor, but what I learned from it was that when my brain is going walkabout, it is possible to keep in touch by focusing on a physical sensation. I was able to talk myself down through a conversation with my senses.

Just as the sensation of a cold steel bar kept me from losing my nerve completely when I was stuck in the lift, it is this feedback from a particular sensory stimulus that can keep our partner on track when they are in danger of being swallowed up by invading overload and fragmentation. It allows them to take refuge in focusing on the one sense that the brain can still process and from which it can draw meaning. This can work through any of the external senses – vision, sound, touch – or through internal feedback (such as, for the schoolboy who draws engines, the feeling of security derived from an image of railway lines that control the direction of movement) but it is always one that is significant enough to pin down attention and hold it.

In an effort to build herself a system she can understand, Amy constructs herself a virtual village in the sand tray. This she can control, but she does so in a curiously detached way; she is the organiser of a 'safe' system. When her teacher offers her new and attractive miniature dolls to incorporate they are swiftly rejected since they are not part of her schema. This draws a sharp distinction between play in a virtual world – one that can be controlled – and actual play, where we can at least potentially cross the boundary between self and other in open-ended exploration. The tactic is to organise rather than participate and the purpose to

---

29  Williams D (1994) *Somebody Somewhere*. London: Doubleday, p99.
30  Gerland G (1996) *A Real Person: Life on the outside*. London: Souvenir Press.
31  Nazeer K (2006) *Send in the Idiots: Or how we grew to understand the world*. New York: Bloomsbury Publishing.

control rather than travel. At a less sophisticated level, repetitive behaviours such as hand flapping are the product of an urgent need to keep a grip on reality, derivative rather than a primary end in themselves, as is so often mistakenly believed.

# Switching the brain off

When the body's self-defence system is triggered by overloading the brain's processing system with too much sensory input, another way for the brain to avoid the consequences of this is to disconnect. The effect is that the person blanks out so that they simply lose touch with their surroundings and have no idea what is happening.

Emerging from a nowhere period and grasping for clues, a young boy on the autistic spectrum looks at the classroom walls around him and sees mathematical symbols. He makes the logical assumption that he is in a maths class. Wrong. What is confusing him is that, while this is the room where he usually learns arithmetic, the lesson currently being taught here is citizenship. His teacher tells him he is naughty because he is not paying attention. She adds that she does not believe him when he tries to explain.

As described in *From Isolation to Intimacy*,[32] this effect of intermittent coherence is expressed by a number of children, all of whom appear to be describing a similar phenomenon. The first keeps saying, 'My head's running away, my head's running away.' His mother is bewildered. 'What does he mean by this?' The second child says that he has his 'funny head' on today. A mother tells me that her grown-up daughter, who experiences severe processing difficulties, describes her brain as being like 'tangled spaghetti', with the odd lucid intervals as 'straight spaghetti moments'.[33]

Yet another child says to his father, 'My head's switched off, switch my head on please,' and his father says that if he makes a downward finger movement as one might to flick a switch, this sometimes helps his son to link up again. It illustrates a principle that can be

---

32  Caldwell P & Horwood J (2007) *From Isolation to Intimacy: Making friends without words*. London: Jessica Kingsley Publishers.
33  Chill A (date unknown) Personal communication with author.

important in practice: that when an autistic partner is stuck in a particular groove and unable to process a particular communication, contact can sometimes be restored by using an alternative mode, (in this case his father answers speech with a gesture).

What all these children are telling us is that they have lost contact with those parts of their brain that enable them to maintain connection with the world around them by correctly processing its sensory input. Literally, they have 'lost the plot', or perhaps more to the point, lost the cognitive plot, with the effect that understanding has broken down. Yet, in spite of this, there is another part of the brain that is able to recognise and express its own dislocation, like the small boy who is able to stand back and say his brain plays tricks on him.

It is evident that in all these cases, even while the person is unable to process incoming sensory information, there is an 'I' who observes their cognitive disorder. As Steven Rose points out in a review of recent books on the functioning of the brain:

> 'Brains are not primarily cognitive devices designed to solve chess problems but evolved organs designed to enhance the survival chances of the organism they inhabit. Their primary role is to respond to the challenges the environment presents by providing the cellular apparatus enabling the brain's owner to assess current situations, compare them with past experience and generate the appropriate emotions and hence actions.
>
> 'However it is not brains that have concepts or acquire knowledge. It is people using their brains. To paraphrase the anthropologist Tim Ingold: I need legs to walk but do not say "my legs are walking". Similarly, I need my brain to think but it is I, not my brain who does the thinking.
>
> 'The mind may need the brain but is not reducible to it.'[34]

---

34  Rose S (2008) In search of the God neuron. *Guardian Saturday Review.* **27 Dec** p8.

# The catatonic response

An alternative way that the brain can switch off when it feels itself becoming overloaded is to become effectively catatonic by locking itself into a repetitive behaviour or phrase. While this is not such a common response, when a young woman in a day centre felt she was becoming too overloaded, she would burst into hysterical crying or laughter, which could last for hours. Her weeping or cackles had an estranged trapped sound and rather than being related to sorrow or humour seemed to be defensive in nature. Nothing was going to get through while she was thus engaged, or rather disengaged from her surroundings.

As our partners become progressively more overloaded to the point where all of their sensory intake breaks up and they are overwhelmed, we need to ask what is so terrible that our partners will do anything to distract themselves and stop this process – bite themselves, tear out their hair or crash their heads against the wall. What is it they are so afraid of? Why do they suddenly appear to tip into self-destruct mode or become hell-bent on hitting, biting and kicking their non-autistic supporters?

When Andre, who quiets himself in a busy pub by drawing patterns in spilled beer, finds that this activity is not sufficient to exclude extraneous sound and 'business', he takes two puppets, which he has carved himself, out of his pocket and enlists their help by making them have a conversation between themselves. If this conversation is interrupted he goes berserk.[35] We can only understand why if we look at what is going on in the brain and autonomic nervous system at this stage.

At this point the brain crashes. The sense of 'I' appears to be overwhelmed (memory of the event may be recovered in retrospect but not always). An unnamed woman with autism tells us that her brain is like a dial-up modem rather than a cable modem: if it is fed too much data, it crashes.[36]

---

35  Nazeer K (2006) *Send in the Idiots: Or how we grew to understand the world*. London: Bloomsbury Publishing.
36  WeirdGirlCyndi (2007) *Sensory Overload Simulation* [online]. Available at: http://www.youtube.com/watch?v=BPDTEuotHe0 (accessed February 2012).

Chapter 2: Whose reality?

# The autonomic storm

The following is an account of an intervention with a child who has encountered circumstances that his brain cannot handle. He has been thrown into an autonomic storm. It is nothing that could have been anticipated and is nobody's fault.

Alister is extremely upset. In crisis, he is lying on the school entrance hall floor, kicking out and bellowing. A number of people are standing over him. I ask them to move back, and start to engage with Alister's sounds. Each time he bellows I respond, lower and with empathy. He is shouting, 'No, no, no thank you'. He kicks out at me but I continue to empathise. After a while he looks at me and it feels as though we are connected for the first time, that he is able to see me. Typically, he starts to test me. He takes off his shoe and slams it down beside him. At this point I know that I have his attention, even if it is expressed in a negative way. Not wanting to get drawn into a custodial and possibly confrontational role, I ignore this and continue to respond to his sounds, turning to his shoe and empathising with its plight (alone on the floor). To my surprise, he picks it up and puts it back on. Seeing that the back of the shoe is not comfortably on, I make an appropriate gesture, running my finger round the heel, and ask if he would like me to help him. He sticks out his foot (instead of lashing out with it) and I ease my finger round the back. I still continue to work his sounds. After a minute or two he gets up, says he is sorry and is ready to go off to his class. As his teacher rightly pointed out, the way he says 'sorry' sounds as if he does not really know what this means in affective terms but knows that this is what he does when he has had a massive outburst. He is aware that it is appropriate to the context without understanding its content.

This intervention tunes in to Alister's extreme distress. It aligns me not with his behaviour but with his affective state, seeking to draw him out by switching his attention from his inner distress to a user-friendly environment outside of himself. I first knew he was engaging at the moment when he took off his shoe and looked at me defiantly; he was starting to test me. At this stage he began to relate to a world outside his 'tantrum' but typically needed to test it. (In order to use this approach one needs to abandon all idea of control. The child cannot help themselves as adrenalin and cortisol pour through them. Words only increase the stress level. Empathy with their state is essential.)

Intensive Interaction using body language can be particularly helpful when the person is entering the autonomic storm, a time when using speech to try and calm them – 'sit down and quieten down' – simply exacerbates their problems, since what they hear are extra sounds that need processing, adding to the bewildering overload they are experiencing. However, Intensive Interaction should not just be used for crisis control but rather as part of an ongoing conversation which helps the person to know what they are doing.

There are a number of descriptions spoken from an inside point of view of the terminal consequences of this sensory overload. Most graphic are those by Donna Williams[37] and Gunilla Gerland[38]. Both describe what amounts to a major disturbance in the autonomic nervous system. These descriptions are supported by evidence that when the sensory impressions in the brain fragment completely in an 'autonomic maelstrom', this firestorm is accompanied by sweating, flushing, heat, confusion and pain.

For Gerland and Williams, the onset of this is a 'fizzy' feeling in the back of the neck spreading as painful sensations through the spine, 'like screeching chalk on a blackboard', 'cold steel, hard and fluid at the same time', 'sharp clips digging into the spine', 'icy heat and digging fiery cold', 'a silent concentration of feeling, so metallic, spreading out to the elbows.'[39]

Tito Rajarshi Mukhopadhyay tells us that he would find coherence watching the ceiling fan going round and round but that this failed when there was a power failure. 'I could hear my scream exploding all my disbelief and anger.' Later he says:

> *'I would feel my anger in my blood, waiting to be pushed out by a big breath from my lungs. I could see nothing else after that. Nor could I hear anything ... and then,*

---

[37] Williams D (1998) *Somebody Somewhere: Breaking free from the world of autism.* London: Jessica Kingsley Publishers.
[38] Gerland G (1996) *A Real Person: Life on the outside.* London: Souvenir Press.
[39] *Ibid.*

> *into the colour of nothingness, the colour of my waiting scream would spread, like streaks and splashes.'* [40]

Six-year-old William describes the anger box in his chest that opens. Anger spreads up into his head and down his arms into his wrists and knuckles and fingers. As he shows me, his fingers press down his arms. He watches them as they drag down his sleeve as if he was tearing at it. He can do nothing to stop it.

Donna Williams goes further. For her, the disturbance starts with the sensation of lemonade in her neck and spreads throughout her body 'like cracks in an earthquake'.[41] She felt she was suffocating inside her shell of flesh. The word 'die' kept repeating itself (for Lindsey Weekes the word was 'pain, pain, pain'[42]). Eventually, exhaustion overtakes the terror. In addition to her account of her internal sensations, Donna also gives us a graphic account of the effect it had on her.

> *'There was a rip through the centre of my soul. Self-abuse was the outward sign of an earthquake nobody saw. I was like an appliance during a power surge. As I blew fuses my hands pulled out my hair and slapped my face. My teeth bit my flesh like an animal bites the bars of its cage, not realising the cage was my own body. My legs ran round in manic circles, as though they could outrun the body they were attached to. My head hit whatever was next to it, like someone trying to crack open a nut that had grown too large for its shell. There was an overwhelming feeling of inner deafness – a deafness to self that would consume all that was left in a fever pitch of silent screaming.'* [43]

---

40  Mukhopadhyay TR (2008) *How Can I Talk if My Lips Don't Move? Inside my autistic mind*. New York: Arcade Publishing.
41  Williams D (1998) *Somebody Somewhere: Breaking free from the world of autism*. London: Jessica Kingsley Publishers.
42  Weekes L (date unknown) *A Bridge of Voices*. Documentary radio programme. London: BBC Radio 4. Produced by Tim Morton for Sandpoint Programs.
43  Williams D (1998) *Somebody Somewhere: Breaking free from the world of autism*. London: Jessica Kingsley Publishers.

# Maintaining coherence through body language

These horrific but consistent descriptions are of an event that can at worst overtake our partners several times a day. It is unsurprising that they take such drastic measures to extricate themselves. But what is becoming more and more evident is that, as Joshua tells us, when he loses his grip on his ability to process incoming information and as a result, his cognitive pathways, non-verbal communication using body language allows him to keep some sense of connection.[44] As such, it is literally a lifeline to coherence. In a state that Donna Williams describes as 'dying' while still being alive,[45] here is just something to hang on to, something that makes sense.

---

44  Harris J (2012) *Joshua's Planet* [online]. Available at: www.joshuasplanet.com (accessed May 2012).
45  Williams D (1998) *Somebody Somewhere: Breaking free from the world of autism*. London: Jessica Kingsley Publishers.

# Chapter 3

# Spaced out

## The singing bowl

At first I think it's a pestle and mortar: a silver bowl with its rim turned in, globe-shaped and inlaid with symbols, of which I recognise the lotus. It sits comfortably in the palm of the hand, while the pestle rolls round its shoulder, gradually picking up to a note of startling purity. This sound, which breathes in the belly of the bowl, is made louder by increasing the pressure of the stick – but loud or soft, the tone rings true.

That was yesterday, but even now the sound carries through my head, not as tinnitus but calm, intense, timeless; a knock on the door from the ether; a calling card from another world.

Like this Tibetan singing bowl, the quality of intimacy does not lie in its dimensions or time. Loud or soft, fleeting or long-term, it reaches in and touches the quick. As the self lays itself open to other, other says, 'Here I am.'

## Lifting the lid

Considering how much trouble we take to fill our lives with trivia and surround ourselves with elaborate self-defence systems, the desire to lift the lid and peer outside of the container of our immediate sensory needs may seem surprising. It is not just the urge to establish contact with the world outside ourselves that is deeply ingrained: beyond this there is also the instinct to 'lose ourselves'. In order to understand this benign desire to be free of attachment to the world around us, we need to see it as part of the wider capacity to detach ourselves from the business of our thinking pathways. In order to find ourselves it helps if we learn to facilitate the capacity to float in sensory awareness.

However, we are irrevocably bound into our bodies. According to our personal sensory filter, each one of us is carrying a different picture of the world. The way in which I perceive, the messages that my senses send to my brain (both those from inside my body as well as those from my surroundings) and the way my brain interprets these, determine my responses to my environment and the people in it.

# Switching off

It is difficult to relate to the world if your sensory input is chaotic and signals from both inside and outside of yourself are scary. As previously pointed out, most people on the spectrum take refuge by turning inward to find a coherent sensory stimulus on which they can focus. At least when they attend to this they know what they are doing.

What do we mean when we say that the brain cuts off from the world outside, or 'switches off', both in the autistic sphere and outside it? I want to examine this not so much in neurobiological terms but rather in terms of the effect that it has on us. I want to know the significance of this in terms of relationship, with things and with people, both for those of us on and off the spectrum.

Discussing the sensory distortions experienced by people on the spectrum with a training group, one member, Pat, tells us that she has a balance problem – sometimes her brain 'forgets' to tell her to stand upright. 'It's a light switching off rather than a wave of sensation … The problem is with the thinking, it's frightening.' This difficulty is mitigated by climbing:

> 'When I climb well I don't think – if I start thinking I fall off ... I hang on to reality by sensing touch when I climb, it's intuitive. I do it automatically; when I am really in it, part of it rather than outside it, there is a loud silence.'

Pat's story suggests that she has problems with her vestibular/proprioceptive system (periodically she is not receiving enough stimuli from her balance organ and messages from her muscles and nerves in her body to her brain, to tell her where she is and what she is doing) and this incoherence is affecting her ability to stand upright. The more she tries to analyse and correct this, the more she gets conflicting messages which she is failing to process. Her muscles tense and her brain becomes clogged: 'it's frightening'. When she climbs, this instability is compensated for by the very powerful muscular sensations she gains by hanging on with the weight of her body pulling on her hands and legs. At least these are strong enough to get through to her brain. By focusing on these sensations Pat can organise and carry out motor movements that are otherwise impeded by tensions induced by unprocessed thinking. She does not need to think in order to move. Feeling her movement frees her from fear.

# The loud silence

Pat speaks of the 'loud silence' when everything comes together and it is this loud silence that intrigues me. As a 14-year-old child I am put into bat in a house rounders game (last, because I am hopeless at games but someone is needed to make up the team). I stand at the base trying to take on board what I have to do – hit the ball and run round the circuit outside the posts. Quick terror. Everything blanks out. Aroused from visual paralysis by a thwack, I return to consciousness and watch the ball soaring away in a high arc through the chestnut tree on the boundary, accompanied by a snow-shower of little white petals. I run – cheers. Run – again, cheers. The game is won. Encouraged by my burgeoning popularity, I grasp the bat and place myself firmly sideways to the bowler in a position that will continue this streak of brilliance. Alas no, as soon as I start thinking about what I am doing, spontaneity is lost, gone, never to be repeated.

Apart from the postcard clarity of the scene, what remains most vividly is the feeling of dissociation, the 'loud silence' contingent to apparent absence but also to enhanced physical co-ordination and response.

## Sacred texts and instruction manuals

So what happens when we switch off our analytic brains? What effect does this have on our ability to relate to the world around us? The experience of damping down the analytical processes and the accompanying inward focus is a wheel that has been reinvented over and over again in different contexts, and which potentially invades all corners of our lives. It has nothing to do with unintelligence or an inability or refusal to think, neither is it a state that can be forced. All that can be done is to put oneself in the way of it with an attentive disposition. In this context it is interesting to compare the following extracts from accounts chosen at random from completely different texts, in no particular historical order. (The attribution is deliberately separated from the quotations and the sources are listed at the end of this chapter.)

1. 'Focusing on the present moment, effortless merging of action and awareness.'
2. 'In the midst of silence, the secret word was spoken unto me.'
3. 'Heightened state of consciousness.'
4. 'The words, "peak", "flow", "perfect moments", "mindfulness", "let", are not generally associated with effort.'
5. 'Mindfulness is a calm awareness of body functions, feelings and content of consciousness … meditative absorption should be combined with mindfulness.'
6. 'Those practicing mindfulness realise that thoughts are just thoughts and one is free to let them go when one realises that they may not be an absolute truth and so be free to live life without getting caught in its commentary.'
7. 'Gazing into the heart of the Divine Darkness.'

8. 'Rapid movement or sudden onset/offsets, produced a "feeling" or "knowing" that some event had occurred even though it was not "seen".'

9. 'A cloud of unknowing. It can be penetrated if one has in thy will a naked intent unto God.'

10. 'Excellence is achieved by letting yourself go and not identifying with illusory aspects. At a certain moment there is a unity of body, soul and breathing. You forget yourself and others. You're not here, you're not there, you are everywhere.'

11. 'Of God Himself can no man think, and therefore I would leave all that thing that I can think and choose to my love that thing that I cannot think. For why, He may well be loved but not thought. By love may he be gotten and beholden; but by thought never.'

12. 'A state of consciousness where the mind is no longer dominated by any thought patterns. If the mind is allowed to randomly travel from one thought or emotion to the next, it does not possess the ability to focus keenly.'

13. 'There is no sense of where and no sense of who – there just is … in there you just go.'

14. 'Man is a thinking reed but his great works are done when he is not calculating or thinking.'

15. 'Athletes in most sports know that their peak performance never comes when they are thinking about it … He is conscious but not thinking … it just seems to happen … The hot streak continues until he starts thinking about it and tries to maintain it. As soon as he attempts to exercise control he loses it … But can one learn to play "out of mind" on purpose? How can you be consciously unconscious? A better way of saying it is that his mind is so concentrated, so focused, that it is still. It becomes one with what the body is doing and the unconscious or automatic functions are working without interference from thoughts. Thinking too much produces tension and conflict in the muscles. Focusing on the seams of the ball rather than on making contact. (Thus fully occupying the thinking brain.) Effortless effort.'

16. 'Be non-judgmental. Feeling where it is, is knowing where it is. As the player finally lets himself observe with detachment and interest, he can actually feel what he is doing and his awareness increases.'

17. 'It's given – we do not feel like taking the credit, rather we feel fortunate.'

So the literature continues across seven centuries. Some of these quotations are from instruction manuals and some from sacred texts. Their authors range from mystics and contemplatives to scientists; from people on the spectrum to sportsmen, artists, writers, Samurai, Zen masters and hunters. While some are easy to assign, others are not so easy to pick out. What they all have in common is that attention is directed away from the brain's thinking processes by way of deep focus on the particular, to the extent that the brain's persistent ticker-tape analysis is switched off. During this period there is commonly a feeling of deep calm and integration, coupled with a sensation described as flow or energy, sometimes together with increased physical co-ordination. In context, almost all who write and teach about such states stress the need for practice and self-discipline.

What all of the states described have in common is the paradox of a sensation of dissociation coupled with heightened awareness of both other and ourselves. Total knowing coupled with total self-abandonment. Add to this a sense of awe and the transitory nature of a state that collapses like the proverbial house of cards as soon as we try to articulate it.

However, just because two things look the same it does not necessarily mean that they are. Although these phenomena may have the same 'feel' and also have common features, it would be a mistake to lump together all of these 'out of (analytical) brain' – or 'state of awareness' – states. Rather, they represent a spectrum stretching from the solitary experience of the autistic condition described by Donna Williams (13), through the physical integration in the 'zone' of the athlete (15 and 19), and the 'drink to me only with thine eyes' bonding of the lover, through to the unknowing of the contemplative (9 and 16).

Although there is overlap, one way of bringing some sort of order to the broad spectrum of affective response is to distinguish between the manner in which the dissociated states are brought about.

# Physical activity as focus

First, attention is focused on a particular object or part of an object. The athlete talks about entering 'the zone' to describe a state where extreme focus takes them into a mode where their motor systems function without, or rather beyond, analysis. Unhindered by self-judgmental tensions, they are aware of their performance in a way that feels detached and frequently produces outstanding performances. *The Inner Game of Tennis* by Gallwey (an American tennis coach) describes his realisation that telling his students what to do sometimes confuses them and makes them less competent rather than more.[46] His interest in Zen leads him to understand that by overloading his students with instructions he is adding to conflicting tensions so that they play less fluidly. When he switches to asking them to focus acutely on the particular, for example, the seams of the ball or the end of the racket, rather than where the ball is going to bounce, there is a marked improvement in their ability. Trying to work out what is going to happen inhibits their performance. Zeroing in on such a narrow target dampens cerebral activity.

An extreme example of such specificity is the behaviour of the autistic brain in full flight into its inner world. In the face of overwhelming sensory invasion, with its terrors of overload and autonomic chaos, the brain focuses exclusively on a particular object or behaviour. In order to make comparison with other affective dissociations, I return to Donna Williams' account of her sensory retreat, where she describes so vividly the 'grip and grab' of an inner state where, having shut down the processing system, the brain is no longer facing continuous hostile challenge.

> *'As a very young child, I discovered the air was full of spots. If you looked into nothingness, there were spots. People would walk by obstructing my magical view of nothingness … my attention would be firmly set on my desire to lose myself in the spots … I learned eventually to lose myself in anything I desired – the patterns on the wallpaper or the carpet … the repetitive hollow sound I got from tapping my chin. Even people became no*

---

46  Gallwey WT (1986) *The Inner Game of Tennis* (2nd edition). London: Pan Books. in association with Jonathon Cape Ltd, pp16–17.

> *problem … I could look through them until I wasn't there, and then, later, felt that I had lost myself in them.'*[47]

Explaining her poem 'Nobody Nowhere', Williams describes what it feels like in her inner world:

> *'It can be total withdrawal into your self when the whole world is replaced and made redundant and you have every relationship with your own self that you could have with people in the world and they don't matter any more.'*

She goes on to tell us what it feels like:

> *'Sometimes people live in there in fear, not in freedom – you can visit in freedom but if you are compelled to live there you live in fear.'*

> *'In a world under glass*
> *you can let the world pass*

> *… For the world can grow cold*
> *in the depths of your soul*
> *where you think nothing can hurt you*
> *until it's too late.'*

The poem ends with a chilling image:

> *'Run and hide to the corners of your mind*
> *alone like a nobody nowhere.'*[48]

While the boy in *A is for Autism* tells us that he likes drawing trains, 'because they are interesting', his voice as he describes what he is doing is detached and unengaged.[49] It is in his eye and hand that we observe focus; he is totally absorbed and lost in his fixation. Attention to his talent is a defensive ploy to keep the world of sensory overload at bay – nevertheless, he is spaced out.

---

[47] Williams D (1998) *Nobody Nowhere: The remarkable autobiography of an autistic girl.* London: Jessica Kingsley Publishers.
[48] *Ibid.*
[49] *A is for Autism* (1992) Film. Directed by Tim Webb. Fine Take Productions with Channel 4.

The problem for the person with autism is that they are weighed down by the baggage of fear: fear of the painful physical effects that are the outcome of sensory overload, described as a 'power surge' in the autonomic nervous system. It is difficult for those of us who have not experienced such distorted feedback from the world we take for granted, to understand what it feels like. A fragment of film on YouTube compares an excerpt from the film *Transformers* to the same episode as the (unnamed) autistic author would see it if she was undergoing sensory disintegration.[50] Sounds roar, images break up into anarchic pixels. The effect is terrifying. This chaos is how the environment presents itself – nothing to hang on to at all… life-threatening. So it is easier to switch off the world outside and turn inwards, focusing on a particular sensation, one that does not impinge on the processing system and add to confusion.

In practice, most of us will have walked away from sensory overload. For example, if there is too much noise going on and we feel invaded, or if there are too many people around, we may be overcome by the feeling that we just want to get out. However, we can manage this without catastrophic breakdown of our senses.

# Stalking

So far the focal object has been inanimate; unresponsive, in the sense that although it may enable the practitioner (for example, the tennis player) to modify their response, the object itself does not alter. Attention is on a particular that does not shift, at least not in such a way that requires the observer to change their own focus. But what happens when the focal object is sentient and can reply? Here is Annie Dillard describing the long watch for muskrats in her timeless book *Pilgrim at Tinker Creek*. The hunter stalks her prey, centring herself so that she becomes one with her surroundings. But her quarry can respond and its fluid reaction has an effect on the hunter, modifying her responses.

> '*Stalking is a pure form of skill, like pitching or playing chess. Rarely is luck involved. I do it right or I do it*

---

50  WeirdGirlCyndi (2007) *Sensory Overload Simulation* [online]. Available at: http://www.youtube.com/watch?v=BPDTEuotHe0 (accessed February 2012).

> *wrong: the muskrat will tell me, and that right early. Even more than baseball, stalking is a game played in the actual present. At every second, the muskrat comes, or stays, or goes, depending on my skill. Can I stay still? How still? ... [A]t the creek I slow down, centre down, empty. I am not excited, my breathing is slow and regular. In my brain I am not saying, "Muskrat! Muskrat! There", I am saying nothing. If I must hold a position, I do not "freeze". If I freeze, locking my muscles, I will tire and break. Instead of being rigid, I go calm. I centre down wherever I am; I find a balance and repose. I retreat – not inside myself but outside myself, so that I am a tissue of the senses. Whatever I see is plenty. I am the skin of water the wind plays over; I am petal, feather, stone.'* [51]

What all of these encounters have in common is extreme attention, but now the target is a variable. Annie, as hunter, must fine-tune her focus into her prey's response. The reference object has become a partner and she enters into conversation. Annie learns from her muskrat partner, who will instantly let her know if she has got it wrong.

## Person to person interaction

Successful partnership, however transitory, is dependent not only on positive feedback but also on attention to (and respect for) negative signals. These tell us where the boundaries of our relationship are. For us, they define not only our partner but (by way of how we see them in relation to ourselves) they also illuminate who we are. This is true of all interactions using body language. For example, when I am working with non-verbal people, negative signals, (which are sometimes subliminally sensed rather than seen), vary from a drop in interest and attention, to incipient signs of aggression when my partner feels I have trespassed on their personal space.

Recent research suggests that when we get too close to our partner the amygdala is activated – the walnut shaped organ in the brain

---
51  Dillard A (1974) *Pilgrim at Tinker Creek*. New York: Harper's Magazine Press.

that acts as an early warning system and plays a key role in emotion.[52] The brain sends out a warning: 'Too close is potentially threatening'. Rather than disengaging totally, I can often manage signs of impending upset by breaking eye contact, stepping back, and taking pressure off the infringement of personal space, even to the point of removing myself from the room but staying in touch through sounds. Meanwhile, I open my arms, indicating vulnerability and to show I have peaceful intent.

Returning to Annie Dillard, her awareness and focus are not lost in a vague mystical cloud but embodied in her senses. She describes the direction of her retreat as, 'not inside' as one might expect, but outward, 'into her senses', to a point of total sentience and identification with all she apprehends.[53]

Wordless person to person interactions embrace the whole gamut of human behaviour, but the ones that I will focus on are those unexpected intimate encounters with strangers. These range from the brief and astonishing to longer-term explorations. Whatever their duration, I have to become an expert at reading body language because this is how I know what my partner is feeling. Maintaining a connection with my wordless partner involves not only paying attention to them but also focusing on the feelings they generate in me – what David Malouf describes in his book *An Imaginary Life*, as 'an interchange of perceptions'.[54]

Malouf describes how the exiled poet Ovid tries to bring language and the benefits of civilisation to a wild child he meets in the woods. When they are both cast out of the tribal area into which Ovid has been exiled, the situation is reversed and he becomes dependent on the non-verbal boy's survival skills.

> *'He is now inducting me into the mysteries of a world I never for a moment understood … a kind of conversation with no tongue, a perfect interchange of perceptions, moods, questions and answers that is as simple as the weather, is in fact the merest shifting of cloud shadows*

---

52 Kennedy DP, Gläscher J, Tyszka M & Adolphs R (2009) Personal space regulation by the human amygdala. *Nature Neuroscience* **12** 1226–1227.
53 Dillard A (1974) *Pilgrim at Tinker Creek*. New York: Harper's Magazine Press.
54 Malouf D (1978) *An Imaginary Life*. London: Vintage.

> *over a landscape or over the surface of a pool as thoughts melt out of one mind into another ... without the structures of formal speech.*
>
> 'We are venturing out into a space that has no dimensions and into a time that may be in human terms just a few minutes but is also an eternity.'[55]

Sometimes these exchanges take place within a very small compass, so that you might feel as though you are examining them under a microscope, illuminated by a spotlight. The effect is of being both observer and participant. What follows is the briefest of intimate encounters, a 'brush-with-a-feather' momentary meeting.

I am standing in the middle of the road bent double, trying to remove a tiny caterpillar from certain death underneath the wheels of passing tractors. It is resisting my attempts to scoop it up on to a broad leaf; it keeps on rolling into a ball and falling off the blade. A car comes up the lane and slows down. The window opens and a woman looks out: 'What on earth are you doing?'. I straighten up. 'Trying to rescue a caterpillar.' She looks down at the tiny creature and then at me. Just for a second our eyes meet and lock. Flow. Overcome by the absurdity of the situation we start to laugh. She pulls gently aside and drives on.

The reason for telling this story is that it illustrates how simple it is to be drawn into intimacy with a complete stranger – in this case through shared humour. I have no idea who she is and we will probably never meet again, but we have been lured into close encounter by a willingness to see the ludicrous side of a situation, even when this involves exposure of our (in this case my) vulnerability. I must have looked silly, backside up as she drove towards me up the hill. My target was invisible to her, as was my purpose, and my dignity was not helped by the hopelessness of trying to intervene in the endangered life of a single wriggling furry larva. What does it matter, one moth more or less? Despite Kipling's delightful story of the butterfly that stamped[56] and ensuing Chaos Theory, any attempt on my part to alter the course of history seems

---

55  Malouf D (1978) *An Imaginary Life*. London: Vintage.
56  Kipling R (1902) The butterfly that stamped. *Ladies' Home Journal.* **October 1902**.

futile. Or is it? Through this momentary meeting two strangers have become coincident. The present has been reshaped. What might have been for her an uninterrupted journey home from shopping, has taken on a particularity, a memory trace. Who is to say what might follow? This memory trace carries a flavour that will remain with me and may in some unknown future influence a choice that I need to make. I am branded by its mark. This is characteristic of intimacy however transitory. We are changed, not the same as before. Losing ourselves in other, whether it is an object, activity or person, we emerge with a minute adjustment to our affective landscape.

# Focus on abstraction

Beyond interpersonal interactions we may dampen our busy cerebral activity by focusing our attention in the direction of an abstract concept, leading ourselves into an affective stream either by accident or intentionally. The watercolour artist Norman Adams launches us into the exploratory nature of such a journey. His attention is focused on the desire to explore beyond our commonly accepted reality, a wash-on-wash kõan designed to penetrate the interstices of the particular and provoke enlightenment.

> *'You look at nature, trying to see what you will never see and that leads you to a kind of spiritual realisation, an understanding of something beyond you. That's what's so exciting about art. The relationship between one colour and another isn't a fact: you can speculate about it. It's an exploration of the area between colours. I think it's a kind of pure spirituality that you can discover by really intense observation and trying to understand nature. It's nothing to do with nature-worship. It's just trying to understand what's out there.'* [57]

As one might expect, referring to what one might term a 'confusion of senses', the artist Tracey Emin describes her experience slightly differently:

---

57  Norman Adams quoted in: Usherwood N (2006) Norman Adams Memorial Exhibition Catalogue: Painting and watercolours 1952–2000.

> *'Sexy moments can be strange; the complete opposite to lying in bed and thinking you have got to clean your bathroom out. I'm talking about the sexy moments that are conjured up by events being on the edge of excitement, nothing lustful or explicit, just a warm sensual feeling of wanting to share. An understanding of a room coming together. Sometimes it happens for me when I am working. Especially painting. An alchemic moment of things joining together, some of the components beyond my control.'* [58]

While this compound sentience has sexual overtones it also has the flavour of 'coming together'. The first time I was aware of this particular combination was in my last year at university. I had been working for some time on a couple of different problems. Unable to reconcile two arguments, I sat back in my chair and rested. Suddenly they slid into each other, dovetailed: a resolution that lay in viewing them from a different and wholly unanticipated angle. It was like one of those impossible cubic puzzles where the wooden shapes have to be turned round and round again, until quite suddenly they fit. We are not sure how they got there but it feels like magic. The whole is achieved: an intellectual integration accompanied by a feeling closely resembling orgasm – mind and body blown.

I should like to place this alongside another of my personal experiences. Together with a friend, I am visiting a folk museum and standing beside a strange configuration set into the grass. On the wall, a notice announces that this is an 'Annalemmic sundial' – one that consists of a dial but has no gnomon (pointer). The 'dial' is a wide arc of numbers, rather like the scale on an old-fashioned weighing machine. The time is told by an exact positioning of oneself relative to the months engraved on a plinth at the centre, straddling the midline, so that one's bulk becomes the pointer. The sky is heavily overcast, so I look back over my shoulder to see if a break is likely, trying to estimate where my shadow should fall. The cloud draws apart and for a brief moment, a faint line falls between three o'clock and four.

---

58  Tracey Emin (2007) My life in a column. *The Independent*. **4 September 2007**.

'Quick, what's the time?'

'Ten past three.'

Illumination! It works. For this second, I am at the centre of things but not 'I' as separate – an observer – but as 'part of': pivot, grounded self. Curiously, now that I am the hub and have the potential for telling any time, time itself has become irrelevant. In contrast to my alarm clock, with its high-heeled, click-clack promenade, this sundial is apophatic, a timepiece liberated from its busy beat, delivering in silence; its end message is the absence of light. I am both empty and full, single-pointed. Everything has come together. I just am. All my senses are totally absorbed in a common purpose. One and one make one: psychologically you cannot slide a piece of tissue paper between me and my experience.

The busy brain is stilled as we perceive ourselves engaging not just 'with' other (be it object or people) but also, 'in' other than ourselves. With all our senses focused in other we are in a state of heightened perception, characteristically involving intense attention, everything coming together in the present and a sense of almost being suspended in a different dimension – Tracey Emin's alchemic moment. At the needle-point of sensory focus we set aside thinking, and in the process become fully attentive to both other and an enhanced sense of self.

# Emptying the mind

Finally, in the spiritual sense we may deliberately seek the goal of 'being in being', a state that is pursued through the practice of emptying the mind, either indirectly through use of techniques such as Zen, the practice of mindfulness or the use of a candle in meditation, or directly as in forms of contemplative prayer, where any thoughts that arise are acknowledged and laid aside.

So the question arises as to whether, each new time the revelation is unveiled (for that is what it feels like), are we simply relabelling our yearning for the dyadic state when we know nothing but just are? Possibly – but this is not necessarily reductionist. The brain is not completely blank; parts of the temporal lobe are activated during meditation, suggesting that although we may not be consciously thinking, our brains are nevertheless actively engaged.

If there is a spiritual principal (or principle), then it has to incarnate somewhere and somehow. Michael Reiss is 'sure that there will be a biological basis to religious faith. We are evolved creatures and the whole point of humanity is that we are rooted in the natural world'.[59] Beyond rhetoric and ritual, this connection comes alive in the work of the 14th century mystic Meister Eckhardt: 'In the midst of silence there was spoken within me a secret word.' ('In the middle of silence, Christ was born into the ground of my soul.')[60]

However, all the time we are caught up in a struggle for words, especially now that we can no longer assume a common cultural reference library, particularly in the sense of what engages us as sacred, our metaphors may not speak to each other, nouns that have been devalued and debased – such as 'ecstasy' – are inadequate or seem 'over the top'. We lack tools to dissect our unknowing. However, we can to some extent walk into it indirectly when we talk about the empirical effects such experience produces in us. These can be and frequently are life-changing. It is not that I have learned something but rather that something has been added. My template has been altered, the relationship is internalised and I am not the same as before. They have become in me and I in them. I am held in the delicate balance between recipient and instigator, and I am grateful.

To bring us back to the earth, and more specifically the tennis court, the feeling of being caught up in a stream of affective awareness is also expressed by our novice (17). However, this describes not just total focus on an unchanging sensory input but on the moving goalposts of an interactive relationship.

Apart from the difficulties of description, such enlightenment is not easily taught. That attained by self-help runs the risk of superficiality (in the sense of knowing about, rather than experiencing) and sometimes of inflation of the self. All we can do

---

59  Reiss M (2009) We are born to believe in God. *The Sunday Times.* **6 June**.
60  Eckhardt M (1979) *Sermons and Treatises.* Vol 1. MO'C Walshe (Trans and ed) London: Watkins Publishing.

is learn to empty our minds, usually but not always, with the help of techniques that focus attention on the sensory world, or with the interventions of a master.

Alternatively, we can hold ourselves open, allowing ourselves to be jolted from one mode to another by using conjunction of the incompatible, the impossible and the absurd. For example, if we return to Pat who is able to quieten fearful thoughts by focusing on the sensations of climbing, what on earth does she mean by 'loud stillness'? The words are a logical contradiction and yet, in another way, extremely evocative. Pure Zen: it evokes resonant feeling in me. Now I know where Pat is and can share her experience in a way that is raw.

# Building the bridge

The affective landscape stretches away into infinity and so far we have only dipped in and out. Our present inquiry is to look at how we can bring the skills of affective attunement into our relationships with other people, especially those on the autistic spectrum. Can we build a bridge between our two worlds in a way that will have meaning for them? Can we have Tracey Emin's alchemic moment when everything comes together, not just in ourselves but as a shared experience? And if we are successful, what will this experience of intimacy mean for our partners, what will they get out of it?

# Brief intimacy

Before going any further, I want to pare down what I mean when using the word 'intimacy' since, like 'feeling' it has a number of different flavours. At one end of the scale we have an intimacy that pertains to friendship, one that has matured like an old, well-loved jacket and has the label 'comfy' sewn into its collar. With you I am at ease. I know that you know all about me as I know about you; we do not have to pretend anything to each other. We can depend on each other, predict each other's responses and operate as a team. If you need help, I will be there for you and if I am in need, I know I can turn to you. This is the fullness of relationship. In a world that

Chapter 3: Spaced out

is biologically hostile, I am prey to the dangers that surround me and will need allies to survive.

However, in the context of this book I shall set aside both long-term relationship and also sexual closeness, (which, together with the drive to nurture, have different biochemical ancestries, each having evolved separately to enable the different requirements of mating, pair-bonding and parenting [61]). The intimacy that I am looking for is rather different and characterised by a curious juxtaposition of surprise and togetherness. An encounter may be measured in minutes, perhaps seconds: a lit flare that retains the particular landscape it illuminates even when its light has faded, imprinting a flavour that is timeless, and which can be revisited long after those caught up in its dazzle have parted, an ember that will glow in the mind when we blow on it.

I did not plan to meet you in this way. It is as if we have slipped by chance into a wordless mental clinch, but one that is the opposite of merger, since I am neither subsumed into you nor you into me, we retain ourselves. Now that we have fallen into each other's minds, 'becoming' in the pool without end, we are both nakedly aware of 'other than ourselves' while remaining self-aware.

At its most fruitful, such brief intimacy is an exploration of a shared mind, a reciprocal and dynamic resonance, which like a verbal conversation follows its partner. In essence it is exploratory and full of wonder. To some extent it follows the rules of a verbal conversation, exchanging active and passive roles. It rarely involves touch; if this were to arise it would be a distraction – although sometimes it can be part of the resolution, a hug coming down from the mountain rather than an orgy on the summit. In mutual dedication we have fallen into each other's minds. At this moment in time we do not exist for the world outside.

Looking for intimacy is rather like seeking the proverbial crock of gold. In any search for such closeness, my desire is in itself a stumbling block: the end of the rainbow is over the next hump. In personal terms I cannot set up such a meeting since what I might be looking for is as yet unknown to me. I can prepare the ground

---

61  Fisher H (2004) *Why We Love: The nature and chemistry of romantic love.* New York: Henry Holt and Co.

by opening the mind and paying attention to its messages, but with people it is not until I stumble into such an encounter that I shall recognise it for what it is. In practice, most mind-meetings are accidental rather than a matter of choice. Quite often with total strangers they arise when we are least expectant. An off-the-cuff remark resonates, opens a door and we find ourselves in a landscape that is both familiar and yet seen through new eyes. We have lost attachment to the world around us. We literally find our base in the other, both losing and finding 'me' in 'not me'. The gateway is through sharing sensory experience rather than cognitive exploration.

# Conversations

This is my experience – all very well for me, but when it comes to conversations (wordless or verbal) with people with autism, one might reasonably ask how it is that I can be certain that this currency of affect is also valid for my partner and not simply a projection on my part. Do they really feel the relationship of exchange, the wonder and synchrony? Or is it just that I feel this and imagine that my partner does too?

Once again it is Donna Williams who clarifies this in her film *Jam Jar*. Walking with her partner on a beach, they listen to the squelching sounds they are making when they press their feet into the wet sand. She says: 'Now it is not just me in my world, but me in my world and him in my world.'[62] If we want to share the affective state with our partner, we are going to have to enter their sensory world, focusing our attention on what has meaning for their brain.

Amazingly, whether it is manifest through smiles, engagement, or sheer wonder, almost every intervention that uses a person's body language to communicate with them culminates in psychological closeness. Through intimate attention something is exchanged. This is just as true of partners on the spectrum as those who are not, although in the case of autism, the change is sometimes more dramatic. We move in uncharted territory.

---

62   Williams D (1995) *Jam Jar*. Film. Fresh Film in association with Channel 4, UK.

Let us meet Jeff, who is completely withdrawn, and Bill, whose defences against the sensory avalanche in his head take the form of destructive rages directed both at furniture and his support partners. Jeff has no speech, Bill has a few learnt phrases. Both have been diagnosed as being on the autistic spectrum.

In addition to his autism, it is clear that Jeff also has a severe learning disability. He appears to have no contact with the world beyond a single act of self-stimulation, a brain-body conversation, where the brain sends a single 'to do' message to the body and the body sends feedback to the brain confirming that it has done whatever it is. His head is sunk on his chest. He sits in his armchair rhythmically scraping what remains of the plastic cover of the arm with his forefinger. This is all he does. I sit beside him and place my hand near his. When he scratches, I scratch back. He scratches, I scratch, he scratches, I scratch. I continue in his rhythm for some time until I am aware that he is now holding back, waiting for my reply. He is no longer on his own. I have become part of his activity and he wants to know what I will do.

Variation creeps in as both of us start to introduce different rhythmic combinations and wait for the other's response. After a while I scratch the rhythm on his sleeve. He withdraws. We sit in attentive silence… then he very tentatively stretches his arm out and takes my hand. I hold it for a little while. Next his thumb presses mine. I press back and he repeats his overture, this time pressing my index finger. We move from finger to finger, a digital stroll, press, pause, answer, move on, thumb to index, index to middle, middle to ring and ring to little; each fingertip explored adds to our understanding of an 'other' that is no longer separate from self. We are totally engrossed, not only in each other's responses, but in the otherness that has become in ourselves. After about 20 minutes Jeff raises his head, looks at me and we are wrapped in each other's smiles. Contact is so simple an act. What else can we give each other but ourselves?

Unlike Jeff, who is completely passive, Bill is described to me as extremely dangerous. In his despair he breaks up furniture, so his room is empty except for a chair and a mattress. Bill is having a bad day when his key worker takes me to see him. He is shouting and banging the walls. His key worker opens the door and (not wanting to invade his personal space, and at the same time making it clear by my body language that I am not going to add to his distress by increasing the amount of stimuli he has to process), I stand outside the threshold of his room and point, asking 'May I come in?' and wait for his reply. To my surprise Bill says 'yes'. I take a step over the threshold and stand still, giving him time to assimilate my movement. After a few minutes I point to the chair and ask if I may sit down. Again he nods. He resumes shouting and then bellows at us, 'Stupid faces, silly noises'. There is something about the way he says this that suggests he is simply repeating what has been said to him in his past, that it falls into the category of learnt speech. One can hear the voice of the person who shouted this at him. (His present placement, which is person-centred and caring, does not in any way reflect his past history in a series of unsatisfactory and negative homes.) I pull a face and answer him, 'Don't worry, I can make stupid faces too.' He stops in his tracks, looks at his key worker for reassurance, goes over to him, puts his arms round him and says, 'I like you' and then comes to me and does the same.

In spite of the differences in their behaviour and cognitive capacity, what these encounters with Bill and Jeff have in common is that during our interaction, attention has shifted from solitary self-stimulation to a shared conversation, be it with or without words. The change in behaviour tells us that our trust is mutual. The focus of our attention has shifted and we become interested in each other rather than locked into ourselves.

# References: Sacred texts and instruction manuals

Here are the references for the quotations on pages 42–43.

1. Ravizza K (1977) *A Subjective Study of the Athlete's Greatest Moment in Sport: The zone.* Publisher unknown.

2. Eckhardt M (1979) *Sermons and Treatises.* Vol 1. MO'C Walshe (Trans and ed) London: Watkins Publishing, pp6–7.

3. and 4. Young J & Pain M (1999) The zone: evidence of a universal phenomenon for athletes across sports. *The Online Journal of Sport Psychology* **1** (3) 21–30.

5. and 6. Mindfulness. *Wikipedia* [online]. Available at: http://en.wikipedia.org/wiki/Mindfulness (accessed April 2012).

7. Ruusbroec J (1985) JA Wiseman (Ed) *The Spiritual Espousals and Other Works*. New York: Paulist Press.

8. Weiskrantz L (2007) Blindsight. *Scholarpedia* **2** (4) 3047 [online]. Available at: http://www.scholarpedia.org/article/Blindsight (accessed April 2012).

9. Anon. *The Cloud of Unknowing and Other Treatises by an English Mystic of the Fourteenth Century. With a commentary by Father Augustine Baker, O.S.B*. DJ McCann (Ed) (1924) London: Burns Oates and Washbourne.

10. Sage A (2009) Boules, Zen and the art of boules: Buddhism adds spirit to sport. *The Times*. **24 August.**

11. Anon *op. cit.*

12. Shaw S (1999) *Samuri Zen*. Newburyport, MA: Redwheel/Weiser.

13. Williams D (1995) Jam Jar. Film. Fresh Film in association with Channel 4, UK.

14. Herrigel E (Suzuki DT) (1953) *Zen in the Art of Archery*. New York: Pantheon Books.

15, 16. and 17. Gallwey WT (1986) *The Inner Game of Tennis* (2nd edition). London: Pan Books in association with Jonathon Cape Ltd.

# Chapter 4

# Body language and conversation

## Intensions

On the first day I started work in what was then known as a hospital for the mentally handicapped, I was afraid. Looking back, I can see that although some of the people who lived there were easily upset (and often had good reason to be) my fear was largely irrational and stemmed from being unable to read people's body language. I did not recognise what their faces were saying, or that an arm being suddenly flung up might indicate fear or muscular spasm rather than threat. This unpredictability bred uncertainty as to people's intensions and I felt threatened. I did not know what they would do next.

We all need to know the intensions of the people we are with and it wasn't many days before I realised that this was the same for the people I was working with; they found it equally difficult to read my intentions. When I raised my arm, was I going to hit them? This was a possibility which at that time was sadly an all too familiar part of their lives.

Since communication is a two-way process, as well as being able to read other people's body language I need to be aware of what my body language reveals to my communication partner about how I feel. This is particularly important in the context of establishing trust between us, since our body language is far less able to practise deception than our spoken thoughts. I want to know if someone is friendly or ill-disposed, and navigating the tricky passage between friendliness and hostility, are they sincere? Do they mean what they say? Even if I make a conscious decision to conceal how I feel, my body language is likely to betray me.

# Interpretations

So what do we mean by body language? Surely it's obvious – isn't it 'what a person does'?

But it is not necessarily that simple, since communication involves at least two parties, and for various reasons we are not always very good at attending to and interpreting what other people are doing. Very often we see what we expect to see and reject what does not fall within the parameters of our expectations or what we think is important. We also need to understand that body language is expressed in different ways that derive from a number of sources – all the significant features of alternative sensory landscapes.

To illustrate how interpretations of body language can alter over time, I want to start with a brief historical excursion.

# Feeling insecure

In 1750 a father writes to his son who is on Grand Tour,[63] advising him on how to behave and begging him that though he may smile he should never be seen to laugh as, 'It is a disagreeable noise and occasions a shocking distortion of the face'.[64]

Why does his father distinguish in this way between laughter and smiling? Reaching back further, the writer of The Book of Ecclesiastes tells us: 'Laughter makes fools of the wise man,'[65] the

---

63  The Grand Tour was a cultural tour of Europe and educational rite of passage popularly undertaken by upper-middle class European gentlemen from the latter half of the 17th century until rail travel in the 1840s made such European journeys accessible to many more people.
64  Chesterfield, Earl of (1929) *Letters of Lord Chesterfield to His Son.* New York: J M Dent & Sons, Everyman's Library.
65  The Book of Ecclesiastes, Chapter 6.

qualitative difference being that whereas smiling is self-contained, within our grasp, when we laugh we are carried away, opening ourselves up to sharing with others, and thus to a state of exposure and vulnerability. We are no longer in total control of ourselves; we have walked off the end of the pier and are at the mercy of the waves of circumstance. At one time or another we have probably all experienced the lurch of disconnection when a joke we have made falls flat. But at the same time, if the person with whom we share an absurdity picks up the humour, we know we are with someone we can trust. We immediately feel close to them.

Lord Chesterfield continues his comments with a description of men who are ill at ease in company:

> *'They adopt a number of tricks to try to keep themselves in countenance, some put their finger in their nose, others scratch their head, others twirl their hats ... behaviours that become habitual.'* [66]

Perhaps hat twirling is less common these days. Nevertheless, although feeling insecure in a social setting appears to be a minor dilemma, in terms of affective ancestry it harks back directly to a much more threatening situation – that of being unacceptable to the biological group we aspire to and which we feel our survival depends on. The response of an outsider in such circumstances is to seek confirmation through repetitive physical stimuli, to self-mother. If we cannot get reassurance from a social context, we look for it within ourselves. For our autistic partners, struggling to draw sense from a life in which they are sensory outcasts, repetitive self-confirmation may be the only consistently identifiable feature in their lives. However, we must always remember that the repetitive behaviours that are thought to be such a feature of autistic self-stimulatory behaviour are secondary, in the sense that they derive not so much from the 'buzz' they provide as from the desperate need to maintain coherence, to bring order to a non-sense experience.

In this context, we may be led badly astray if we try to interpret repetitive behaviours within the context of our own logic. Since he has apparently made a choice, a man who repeatedly points to his cup is given water every time, resulting in him having to be taken

---

66  Chesterfield *op. cit.*

to hospital with severe salt imbalance. It turns out that his request is not for water. He is pointing to the picture of Superman on his cup. When his cup is broken, his health is restored.

# Body language as an expression of feeling

Whether we are good at it or not, we are all body language watchers. In our everyday exchanges, consciously or not, we monitor the body language of others continually since it informs us of meaning. Think of the difference between 'that's funny' (ha-ha) – wide open face, smile, crinkled eye muscles, and 'that's funny' (odd/peculiar) – chin drawn back, lips down at the corners, eyebrows frowning.

Body language tells us not just what people mean and what they are doing, but also how they feel. As we register this, we know if they are still onside or not. This knowledge relates to survival behaviour, measuring responses in terms of, 'Does this gesture or attitude indicate a response that is good or bad for me?' I am always on the lookout for recognition and pleasurable confirmation and I can pick up signs of these from body language.

When an interviewer on the other end of a phone asks how much we use body language in our normal communications, I respond that we use it to monitor our conversation partner's intentions all the time, checking up on what they are feeling. Do their words match up with their facial micro-expressions? I go on to add that this is why telephone interviews are so difficult. I cannot see whether he is fiddling with his pencil and wondering how quickly he can get this woman off the phone. He laughs, so I know he is still with me, but only because the medium that transmits our non-verbal exchange has been redirected from vision to sound and is now unblocked. Without being able to read your body language I am uncertain of your intention. While we may be able to copy one another, we are not having what in any sense can be called a 'conversation' involving affective exchange.

Worse still is the pseudo-intimacy adopted by call centre staff whose script insists that they wheedle themselves into the position of a friend through the technique known as 'synthetic personalisation'. 'Hello Phoebe, how are you today?' strikes a hollow note when we have never met before. As soon as it is recognised, this artificial familiarity has the opposite effect of that intended, one of separation rather than closeness.

## Non-verbal conversations

So what can we get out of non-verbal body conversations?

Walking along a lane, a little girl wearing a bright green jacket splattered with blue leaves toddles down the hill clutching her mother's hand. As soon as she spots me she raises her free arm in salutation. I respond by raising mine and lowering it when she puts hers down. She looks thoughtful and raises hers again. When I answer with the same gesture her face splits into a grin and she repeats the gesture. This time I raise my hand and add in wriggling my fingers at the same time. Now she is really engaged and so am I. No question, we are talking to each other, interacting for the sake of having fun.

Since we have never met before, her first advance is solemn-faced and experimental: 'What happens if I use this greeting to this person?' I answer by imitation, confirming that I have not only received and taken on board her gesture but, perhaps more importantly, that it means something to me. The second time she is more confident since now she knows that what she has initiated will get a response – she has judged it right. However, the third time something unexpected happens. Initially she gets the signal that her brain expects but then, within the context of her expectation, something completely different happens. She perceives a discontinuity and her brain receives a jolt, but nevertheless the signal is a near enough match to be assessed as user-friendly. This small exchange triggers in both of us 'the feeling of mental constraint and release which is the essence of laughter'.[67] Using our body language we have introduced ourselves and found each other to be entertaining company.

---

67    Lubbock T (2008) These paintings are a joke: can modern art be funny? *The Independent* **24 January 2008**.

It does not always work out so well. When I am collecting eggs from a farm further up the road, a slightly older child abruptly terminates an exchange by sticking out her tongue, turning away and stomping back into her house. Quite clearly she does not want to be friends. This burst of defiance does not last, since the next time we meet she keeps her eyes lowered as she hands over my change. We both remember that last time I had unwittingly trespassed too far into her territory.

It is not just actual body posture that is important in these exchanges. Consider the body language of two boxers at the weigh-in, nose to nose, eyeballing for the knock-down stare, challenging each other: 'I am a better man than you are'. This may be contrived for the benefit of the media, but nevertheless offers a completely different scenario to two lovers in much the same position gazing into each other's eyes. There is a marked contrast: hostility versus invitation, no question which is which.

# Me and 'not me'

These wordless but surprising excursions into 'other which is not self' (or 'not me') are extensions of the game of imitation and exchange played between mother and baby. In these journeys the end is unpredictable but the game is nevertheless played within certain rules that render it safe to take part. Even if it seems uncomfortable to think of bonding in terms of neurochemistry, in the dyadic state, mother and child initiate pleasure in each other through positive recognition, confirmation and the feel-good factor this engenders.

In our relationships we are testing the waters each time: sometimes they are good for a swim and at others we flounder. It's all about how we express our feelings to each other through our body language. In essence, body language is the colour of what would otherwise be a black-and-white interaction.

So what do my partners on the spectrum get out of it? It is perfectly true that people with autism cannot read body language under what we who are not on the spectrum consider to be normal circumstances. However, it is also evident to those who practise the approach known as Intensive Interaction, that our partners can and do respond if, first, the brain is not overloaded with sensory inputs, especially those that they may be hypersensitive to, and second, if we use gestures that are part of their repertoire. Under these circumstances our partners will always watch intently, refer back in a relevant manner, reciprocate and introduce related material. Some people are very good, not only at copying but at moving on to extemporise on what has been introduced. When we get it right there is a very marked relaxation of tension in the body posture and facial expressions, which indicates pleasure and relief. Frame by frame analysis of video footage demonstrates that, although the timeline may vary, when we use body language to communicate, eye contact and social responsiveness increase, and our partner moves closer to us.[68]

# Getting started

When I want to get in touch with how my partner feels, I look out for clues as to the way they are talking to themselves. This is expressed through the physical sensory feedback they are giving themselves and their bodily presentation.

First of all, there are movements and sounds made by our partners and ourselves that are largely unconscious. Here there is no intention to communicate with the world outside. For example, we feel our bodies, perhaps give ourselves physical feedback by rubbing our fingers, twiddling our thumbs or, sitting with knees crossed and wriggling our feet. The observer sometimes finds this type of behaviour aggravating – possibly because it points towards self-mothering, indicating a person's interest in themself rather than others – and so it is seen as a barrier to communication. We may feel that there is something about our partner that, while claiming sensory witness, simultaneously excludes us. In a slightly different category are the sounds that people make, the sounds of breathing or the grunts and sighs that, while not intended for communication, relate to anxiety, discomfort, effort or even elation. I shall also be

---

[68] Zeedyk S, Caldwell P & Davies CE (2009) How rapidly does Intensive Interaction promote social engagement for adults with profound learning disabilities? *European Journal of Special Needs Education* **24** (2) 119–137.

looking for rhythms and habitual behaviours and observing the way that these are being carried out, letting the sensations soak into my own body and picking up on clues as to how my partner feels.

Imagine, for example, that while we speak I am fiddling with my car keyring, feeling the keys gently at first but as I become increasingly irritated with what you are saying, I rub them more and more urgently until finally, unable to reach consensus, I slam them on the table and get up. My body is rigid as I snatch my keys sharply, turn away and leave.

With non-verbal people there are many preverbal gestures, attempts to make their needs and desires known to us and to tell us how they feel. For those of us who are verbal, apart from speech there are also rhythms to the way we talk, the 'ums' and 'ahs' that punctuate our speech, and the speed at which we express ourselves, getting faster as we become more tense. These factors are also present in the communication of non-verbal people. In addition, there are our facial expressions and posture, the activities in which we are interested and the way we do these.

However, if I am meeting you for the first time, amongst this plethora of your behaviours I look for a shortcut that indicates where I should start to focus my attention.

# How is my partner talking to themselves?

Even though the brain of our autistic partner may be in turmoil, it is not in the human character to focus on nothing. The brain will keep trying to find a focus. Both personal accounts and individual behaviour suggest that, no matter how scrambled the messages in the brain, our partners are continually searching for meaning, for a pattern that can be interpreted, for coherence. So the key to opening out communication with our non-verbal partner is to look at how they are self-stimulating, to hone our sensory awareness so that we pick up on the feedback they are generating for themselves and particularly the way they are doing it, as this is what tells us how our partner is feeling. At the same time we need to reduce any overloading sensory input that prevents them from reading our body language.

It is not always the most immediately obvious behaviour that offers access to interaction and 'conversation'. A small boy in a wheelchair bangs his table incessantly. Responding in the same way encourages him to bang harder but does not promote interaction. How can we get him to step outside of his inner world and think about what is being offered in a more interactive way? Careful observation suggests that in addition to his noisy behaviour he is mouthing all the time, chewing his tongue and lips. Is this the way he is talking to himself (rather than expressing his frustration to the world outside)? Building on this I try using vibration, providing a stimulus near his mouth that has meaning for him. He becomes deeply attentive, uncurls, sits up and smiles, reaching out in a way that is completely interpersonal. He begins to use delighted sounds to 'talk' to me. In this case, it was the sensations he was generating around his mouth rather than his table banging that he was focusing on.

# Coercion and motivation

In an extreme sense, the consequences of failing to align ourselves with the affective state of a partner are well illustrated in a recent television series that follows the lives of two children with severe autism after they had been the subjects of an approach known as operant conditioning. This therapy, based on a rigid behavioural approach, aims to develop speech using 'reward' and 'punishment' in a way that now seems intrusive and disrespectful.[69] The children were shouted at and physically manipulated until they complied, trained in an extreme form – the justification being that at the end they learned words (but as Alex's brother put it 10 years later, not how to use flexible language). The film shows Alex, 40 years on, walking around, his attention totally fixated on a clothes hanger, swinging it slowly from side to side. Occasionally he glances at his brothers but shows little engagement with them. In an eagerness

---

69  *What Happened Next: The broken bridge* (2008) Television programme. Directed by Robert Reed. London: BBC Four, 29 May 2008.

to force the development of speech, what has been overlooked is the even more fundamental necessity of emotional engagement, the motivation of our autistic partners in a way that is so powerful that they are prepared to lay down their defensive strategies, in order to link up in a meaningful way with the world outside their own.

Rather than coerce the development of speech, I want to motivate my partner so that they will be eager to engage with me. The easiest way to start is to use their non-verbal sounds, whether or not they are intentional, since they will normally recognise these very quickly. These responses increase in volume once the person knows they will get an answer every time they make an initiative. They become more confident.

However, I have to be careful since the person may well exhibit a variety of behaviours, not all of which will give me access to my partner's inner conversation, as the following two stories illustrate.

Jim chats away to himself, waves his arms about and plays with his hands. When his mother responds with his sounds he just talks over her and does not stop. She says she is not having any luck with communication. When I meet him it is clear that he gives himself feedback in a number of ways. Although he was unusually quiet on the day that I saw him, he normally makes sounds, often quite loudly. Today he is grinding his teeth and rubbing his fingers. Sometimes he blows raspberries. In his chair he rocks and taps his foot or both feet on the wheelchair. He places his fingers in front of his face and looks at them. I try combining my responses to these behavioural patterns in different ways, looking for novel combinations of the elements of his language that will have meaning for his brain while at the same time carrying the added value of surprise.

His sounds increase as I rub his hands at the same time as answering his sounds. Later I respond to his teeth grinding by drawing a stick across the ridged surface of his foot rests. He starts to bang his right heel deliberately on the footrest. I answer by holding his leg and tapping back. He then offers his other foot. His attention to our 'conversation' increases and he begins to smile.

A day or two later his mother emails that the family feel that, now Jim knows that his actions will get a meaningful response (blowing raspberries and foot tapping), they are able to communicate with him for the first time. While some might raise the objection that encouraging Jim to blow raspberries and bang his legs is not socially appropriate, what is critical for Jim and for his family is that he has realised that if he does something that is important for him, his initiative will be recognised and he will get an answer that makes sense as it is part of his repertoire. The 'silence chasm' between him and his family has been bridged, and having established the elements of his vocabulary, the way he uses them will tell his family how he feels. For example, what does the vigour with which he kicks his footrest tell us? Is he relaxed or agitated? Most of all, he and his family have made an emotional connection, establishing the bridge between each other, which in spite of years of obviously devoted support, has not previously been possible.

# Are there any rules we can apply?

Towards the end of a seminar a student asks me how in any particular interaction she can know how she should reply. This is an important question couched in the wrong language, since the way we go about replying is not a cognitive act with rules: if my partner does 'A', I must do 'A' or sometimes 'B'. Rather, the mode of response is arrived at through observation and intuition by way of trial and error, the focus being not so much on 'acts' that we or our partners 'do' but on interaction – and the effect we are having on each other. We learn from our partners, watching what they do, responding to the feelings they generate in us and observing what affect our 'answers' have for them. As a general rule, however, I do not so much replicate my partner's initiatives but rather offer a contingent match. This is in the affective sense as well as the physical sense, so that my response is near enough to their behaviour to catch the attention of their brain. I use recognisable elements of their language to tune in to how they feel (but with a soupçon of disharmony).

The reason why this is an effective approach is becoming clearer. In his book *The Decisive Moment*, Jonah Lehrer describes how expected recognition (confirmation) stimulates the brain to produce a small amount of dopamine (the feel-good neurotransmitter) in the nucleus accumbens, but unanticipated confirmation causes a bigger release – three to four times the amount.[70] In fact, we are programmed to look for something new. Our brains are novelty seekers and a desire to move on is a side-effect of the increased pleasure reward. The fact that people with autism exhibit eager behavioural responses to recognised signals presented in an unanticipated way suggests that they also experience such rewards.

## Pitfalls

There are various pitfalls. The first is physical disability, for example, undiagnosed deafness or visual impairment, or incapacity dismissed as part of a general learning disability. It may seem obvious that our responses must be presented within our partner's visual or auditory field – they have to be able to see or hear what we offer. But it is easy to be misled by apparent unresponsiveness due to the inability to receive our signals rather than a disinclination to respond. For example, a man who has tunnel vision may not see the signs made to him if these are outside of his restricted visual field. He may be judged to be 'lazy' because sometimes he responds and sometimes he does not. Staff say that 'he can't be bothered'.

In our eagerness to communicate it is also easy to be lured into the pitfall of trying to premeditate the mode in which our conversation will be carried out, based on previous interventions with partners who appear to be similar. In the sense that we must work in the present, experience can be a snare.

I am trying to engage the attention of a small girl on the autistic spectrum. She hits herself either with her hands or if these are restrained, by lashing out and hitting her head on anything close by. She makes sounds, so I begin by using these to try and get a conversation going but she takes very little notice, continuing to wander about, picking up one toy, dropping it and moving on to the next. (In some ways, when our partner makes sounds it seems to us like the natural way to make contact – a precursor to speech and

---

70  Lehrer J (2009) *The Decisive Moment*. Edinburgh: Canongate Books, p39.

therefore the logical key to communication.) Because I am sure that her sounds are the way in, it is perhaps an hour before I notice that she is playing with her fingers. What her brain is actually listening to – her personal conversation with herself – is not her sounds but the sensory messages afforded by touch and pressure. These are the incoming stimuli she recognises most easily. As soon as I join in and start to press her fingers she becomes extremely thoughtful. She presses back and waits for my response, and gradually comes out of the quilt she has been hiding under. I had made the elementary error of launching in to a predetermined strategy without looking at what was the most important sensory input for her.

## Kick-starting a conversation

On the other hand, if I know that a person makes sounds but they are not doing so at the time of our interaction, it is sometimes possible to kick-start a conversation by using the sounds that I or a support worker has heard previously. It all depends whether the sounds, or rhythms of sound, we make are near enough to ones that are part of the person's repertoire for them to recognise: 'That's my sound but I did not make it'. This shifts attention outwards from the inner world in search of the source. Just as in verbal conversation, either of us may start the ball rolling.

## 'Staring at' and 'gazing into'

As well as speech, we are deeply dependent on eye contact for communication (unless we have a visual impairment). It is not just the eyes but all the tensions in the minute muscles around them that define expression. For the casual onlooker, precisely because it means so much to us, it is possible to misinterpret intention. For example, 'staring at' or 'eye-balling' is not the same as 'gazing into' someone's eyes. On the one hand there is the stare of someone who is fixating on eyes. There is something rigid about this. Like the boxer at the weigh-in mentioned earlier on, there is hostility rather than invitation. Yet under these circumstances I have been told a number of times, 'They enjoy eye contact'. In such situations our partner is using us as an object (even if it is for the very good reason of maintaining coherence) and not as a subject with whom the warmth of affection can be shared. In taking account of one aspect of the body language, that of proximity, we have neglected the hardness or softness of muscular tone, and the inflexibility both in posture and expression.

So, whether or not we are on the autistic spectrum, the way that we present our body language is determined by how we feel. In particular, it is the giveaway as to how calm or tense we are. Since people on the spectrum are unable to filter out what is important from the torrent of incoming stimuli, they constantly feel themselves to be in danger of drowning. Their body language will largely consist of responses to this assault.

## Identification with my partner's feedback

In whatever manner our autistic partners are expressing themselves – through preverbal sounds, repetitive behaviours or fixations – what they have in common is that, in a state of sensory overload, the brain not only recognises their feedback but also identifies with it. It carries an affective charge that helps our partner to feel safe. Seeing, hearing or feeling 'their activities' as sensory input generated from outside themselves, our partner can home in on the physical sensation they obtain from these and, even though they did not make them, use them to know what they are doing.

## What has meaning for my partner?

Wherever I start, I am going to have to learn to pay intimate attention to what it is that has meaning for my partner. However, it is all too easy to fail to make the distinction between overall behaviour and particular behaviour: 'My partner is sitting down', versus, 'My partner is sitting down and their left thumb is scratching their right index finger'. While both are true, the first describes the person's overall position but the second draws attention to the sensory feedback they are giving themselves. This is in effect a conversation being held between the brain and the body, where the brain says to the body, 'Scratch your finger' and the body replies though feedback to the brain, 'Done it'. In addition, there will be subtleties of pressure by which my partner is varying and so adding interest to the conversation they are having with themselves. This is the feedback I have to tap in to in order to get their attention, to switch their brain from monologue into dialogue.

In addition to watching and listening to my partner with all of my senses, I need to cultivate awareness of my own sensory responses to their initiatives – what are these telling me about how my partner feels? This is not a cognitive act on my behalf but rather learning to catch hold of any variation in reflected feeling, often quite subtle – like catching a glimpse of a peripheral flutter behind us in a mirror, an almost subliminal twitch, a knock on the door that alerts the brain to possible change, a signal to be investigated. Even though I may not recognise exactly what is going on, I need to take note of this movement and switch my attention to the feeling generated by any alterations in the tone of my partner's affect.

I want to end this chapter with an account of an intervention that highlights the importance of using observation of body language to isolate the site at which someone is self-stimulating. Kayer is an 11-year-old boy whom I meet in school. He is diagnosed as being on the autistic spectrum. Kayer has speech, can read and write, and is attentive in class, working hard at the tasks he is given and seeming to have a good understanding of their purpose. As seen by his teachers, his main problem seems to be that he is terrified in the playground – as another boy puts it: 'He stands in the corner and won't play with us.' With his back to the wall this corner is the place he feels safe. (In the film *A is for Autism* a child describes the horrors of playtime: children shouting and running about. There is too much to process and it feels threatening: 'I thought I was going to go mad.'[71])

I first see Christoph in class. I point to the chair next to him and ask if I may sit down. He nods, so I sit and watch while he talks to his teacher. After a short while I notice that when he is not immediately engaged in work he moves his fingers along the edge of the table and also rubs the palm side of his thumbs.

---

71   *A is for Autism* (1992) Film. Directed by Tim Webb. Fine Take Productions with Channel 4.

This is the sensory stimulus he uses to talk to himself (just as people who are not on the spectrum sometimes twiddle their thumbs round each other). I ask him if he likes doing it and he politely offers me his thumbs to try it out. I decide to enhance his self-stimulatory signal by using a vibration unit on his thumbs, the site that has special significance for his brain; he clearly loves it. When playtime comes (the point when he would normally make a bolt for his corner), I suggest that we take the vibration unit with us and use it to lure him into sitting at a table in the playground. We sit together and explore the sensations it offers. I tell him that it's called a buzzer and that he is the 'buzzer boss'. Soon another child leans over and asks what we are doing so I suggest to Christoph that he shows the buzzer to her by using it on her hands. I say that he can lend it to her if he wants but that she must give it back as he is in charge. His confidence grows visibly and soon five children have gathered around him, all eager to interact. Then Kayer does something completely new. He looks at the boy next to him, gets up and they start to play a game of chase, both of them laughing. One can see that he is not used to running – his gait is awkward – but even when he momentarily flags, he pulls his shoulders back and starts off again.

In their new book *Making Animals Happy,* Johnson and Grandin, (the American professor who has autism herself), describe the conditions for good husbandry. They suggest that, since how animals feel has neurobiological consequences which will affect their behaviour, their environment should be aimed at activating positive emotions as much as possible and activating negative emotions no more than necessary.[72] Without disrespect to the human condition, in this sense we are all animals and what Grandin and Johnson are saying applies to all of us, autistic or not. I am more likely to be able to co-operate if I feel confirmed than if I feel threatened.

From the point of view of Intensive Interaction, Christoph's newfound ability to relate is directly through vibration: 'You buzz, I answer.' So why is it that using the vibration device with him so radically alters his behaviour in such a short time? The reasons for this are complex and to answer this question we need to think in

[72] Grandin T & Johnson C (2009) *Making Animals Happy: How to create the best life for animals and pets.* London: Bloomsbury Publishing.

terms of a signal that introduces Christoph to an environment that his brain assesses as friendly rather than threatening. In a sensory world perceived as chaotic, such a model aims to reduce frightening circumstances and increase signals that have meaning for the brain – in Christoph's case, strong proprioceptive signals given at the specific location that his body language suggests has the most significance for him. In doing this I am acting on the assumption that his body language initiative (his thumb rubbing), is 'hardwired' in and does not contribute to the sensory overload that is jamming up his processing system.

First, I observe acutely what Christoph is doing, searching for the site of his self-stimulus – the physical feedback he is giving to his brain: in this case, the inner side of his thumbs. I then offer him a matched but enhanced proprioceptive response, one that is powerful enough to capture his attention, shifting his focus to a source of 'his signal' – the one that he focuses on in order to reduce the invading overload of signals from the world outside which he cannot process.

His brain locks in: 'I want this', to the extent that he is no longer overwhelmed by the sensory chaos of the playground. Here is something he can control and also, in his case, one that offers him an opportunity to interact with the other children instead of being terrified by them. When I have to leave, I tell him that his teacher will get a buzzer and that if he is ever frightened he can ask her to let him hold it. This will reduce his fear, not only of things that are happening but also the anticipatory stress of things that may happen, since now he has an escape route.

It is difficult to relate to others if one does not have a clear picture of oneself. This powerful signal seems to anchor Christoph, releasing him from his fear and allowing him to engage with his classmates. It gives him a picture of who he is, a base from which he can move out to form relationships. In a physical sense, it grounds him.

Christoph's newfound confidence lasts beyond periods when he is actually receiving the stimulus. Bearing in mind the tendency of the autistic brain to perseveration, perhaps the powerful sensation of vibration continues after the actual stimulus is removed, so that there is still a tingling in the thumbs on which he can focus.

Or perhaps it is just that he has found a new way to relate to his classmates. It is interesting that, although they have not played before, the boy that Christoph chooses to run off with is one who says he sometimes stands near him in his corner when he is in retreat. Either way, it seems to be a question of balance, trading off a massive increase in meaningful signals against those that the child finds so frightening because they cannot be processed and therefore threaten to tip him into an autonomic storm.

What about the future? It may be that simply knowing that a buzz is available when he is afraid will be enough to calm Christoph's fears – or he may need to actually use it. Alternatively, the brain may habituate so that he succumbs to his terrors again. If this happens it will be necessary to find another source of stimulation and, since the aim is to integrate him with his peers, preferably one that other children will find fascinating. Probably an object that vibrates or possibly an instrument like a guitar, which can be plucked with his fingertips.

It is critical that his play is supervised closely so that Christoph's confidence is not destroyed by having the buzzer removed by another child. He needs to be reminded that he is in charge. While it is important that he has access to the buzzer when he feels he needs it, I would want the teacher to remain in overall charge of it, so that Christoph looks outside himself for the stimulus he needs to deal with the world. If he has unrestricted access his brain may get used to its stimulus and the overall effect could be lost.

The buzzer is not a toy but a vital part of Christoph's 'life support system', enabling him to deal with the outside world. In the long-term future it might be possible to negotiate with him that his friend has a turn being in charge, but this would need to be done under supervision and it would have to be someone he trusted.

However, the conclusion I want to draw from this intervention and many others with partners on the autistic spectrum (even if they are verbal) is that using body language to communicate needs to be part of an adaptive approach that maximises significant signals and reduces fear, making it possible for the individual to find coherence and work out what is going on in their environment.

# Chapter 5

# Mimicry, copying, imitation and using body language to communicate

## Recognition

In the natural world, the difference between acceptance and rejection can be a matter of life and death. In some respects it is also a matter of mathematics. My flock of geese numbers 70. Each gander needs two wives. Apart from a couple who form a gay relationship with alternating dominance, surplus ganders stop eating. Surrounded by lush grass, they separate themselves from the group, fade away and die.

We can translate this into human behaviour. For survival purposes we need to be accepted and liked in order to be included, and to therefore be able to profit from the protection afforded by our chosen social group or groups. However, at the same time we do

Chapter 5: Mimicry, copying, imitation and using body language to communicate

not want to be subsumed by our setting. We need to stand out sufficiently to be noticed, otherwise we shall find it difficult to attract the all-essential partner. This delicate balance is known as Brewer's optimal distinctiveness theory, and essentially asks: how much individuality can we get away with without compromising our group attachment?[73]

Part of the way we manage this is by using body language, especially 'mimicry' – adopting the behaviour of the group – since mimicry promotes bonding. If we are unconsciously mimicked we feel favourably disposed towards the one who imitates us. We are more likely to help pick up spilt pens, to donate to charity or to be generally more co-operative if, unknown to us, our partners have previously been imitating our behaviours, for example, foot tapping or hair touching.[74] It may seem absurd but waitresses are more likely to get larger tips if they repeat an order back to their diners, rather than just walking away to fetch their meal.[75]

This ability to mimic or 'imitate' as it is known by psychologists, is a vital tool in our struggle for acceptance by our carers and peers. If we can't get people to like us, somewhere inside we feel anxious – the surface ripples of a much deeper anxiety relating to our potential survival. We are looking for people we can identify with, who will promote our welfare and with whom we feel safe. Their imitation of us modifies our behaviour and ours, theirs. Provided that people come from a group that we can socially identify with, we become more socially responsive if we are unconsciously mimicked, making us more likeable to our partner. But before we get too locked into the idea of human cohesion, we should note that our behaviour is similarly affected in a positive manner if the one who imitates us is an avatar, wriggling its impersonal foot in response to our restlessness.

It is not just psychologists who are fascinated by the idea of how we come to like and trust each other. The imitation story is also being opened up by contributions from neurobiologists conducting

---

[73] Brewer MB (1991) The social self: on being the same and different at the same time. *Personality and Social Psychology Bulletin* **17** (5) 475–482.
[74] Van Baaren RB, Holland RW, Kawakami K & Van Knippenberg A (2004) Mimicry and prosocial behaviour. *Psychological Science* **15** 71–74.
[75] Van Baaren RB (2005) The parrot effect: how to increase tip size. *Cornell Hotel and Restaurant Administration Quarterly* **46** (1) 79–84.

research with modern brain scanners. From them we are beginning to glean clues as to which parts of the brain are firing and which neurotransmitters are involved when we perform an action. For those of us in practice with people on the autistic spectrum, the most interesting question is how we can link this research with the experiences that we are shown by the people we work with.

When I first became involved with people on the autistic spectrum, 25 years ago, I was informed by a psychologist that I should discount what people with autism were saying about their condition because their brain processes were faulty, so any information we obtained from them was inevitably subject to error.

In practice, this has been a tragic misapprehension. It is only since we started to listen carefully to what people like Donna Williams, Temple Grandin, Gunilla Gerland, Therese Jolliffe and many others are telling us (combined now with graphic film illustrating sensory distortions, which is available on the internet [76]) that we are beginning to get a clear picture, not just of the fact that people with autism have problems with cognitive processing (what we can see in them), but the extent of the pain, confusion, sensory distortions and autonomic distress they are suffering (what they are experiencing). What does it feel like to be the subject of an autonomic storm? The metamorphosis is described by a man on YouTube as his 'autistic werewolf tantrums'. He feels taken over, as indeed this is the condition in his brain, which is being flooded by a tidal wave of autonomic distress.[77]

So can we use imitation to communicate with our autistic partners, especially as it is normally supposed that those with autism do not recognise and connect with what is going on around them?

A borrowed list of ways that we unconsciously mimic each other includes, on the one hand, behaviours related to speech, such as accent, voice tones, pauses, rates of speech and syntax, and on the other hand, non-speech related behaviours, such as posture, mannerisms, moods and emotions. Both the person who mimics

---

76 WeirdGirlCyndi (2007) *Sensory Overload Simulation* [online]. Available at: http://www.youtube.com/watch?v=BPDTEuotHe0 (accessed February 2012).
77 Autisticwerewolf (2008) *W-06 Part 1: Do not let autistic tantrums/meltdowns take centre stage!* [online]. Available at: http://www.youtube.com/watch?v=qduQ2gwVnMY (accessed April 2012).

and the recipient are normally unaware of their subliminal interchange.[78]

However, the approach I use is more than mimicry, imitation or copying (although it contains elements of these). Just as in spoken language, I try out a number of different combinations and responses that tune in to my partner's body language. In particular, I shall focus on the sensory feedback that my partner is using to talk to themselves – some feature of their body language that is hardwired in and so does not require elaborate processing.

John is bellowing and biting himself. Because screaming loudly involves putting pressure on the neck muscles, I try putting pressure on his shoulder every time he bellows, a technique that is sometimes effective, but not in John's case. So after a few tries I switch to visual copying, putting my hand in my mouth and pretending that I am biting it, echoing his sounds (more quietly) at the same time. After three bellows, he begins to come out of his world. He looks up, his voice lowers and his eyebrows rise. He gives a sort of gulp and reaches out for his book. Thereafter, every time he looks up I make a growling noise in my throat, so that he begins to realise that if he makes a sound he will get an answer. We start to have a conversation. His attention has shifted to the world outside himself, rather than on his internal distress. His support workers find that this is an effective technique that works every time he starts to become distressed. At the same time we examine his environment to see if we can reduce the triggers for his distress so that he is not so frequently upset.

The reason I try pressure first, rather than direct imitation, is that when a person is so deeply entrenched in their distress, and in this case expressing it through sound, they may not always notice a visual response. However, John responds to straight mirroring.

Sometimes it is more effective to use responses in an alternative mode.

I am working with Nigel in his classroom. One of his classmates, David, is desperate to join in and keeps on coming back and interrupting our conversation. However, when it comes to David's

---

[78] Van Baaren RB, Holland RW, Kawakami K & Van Knippenberg A (2004) Mimicry and prosocial behaviour. *Psychological Science* **15** (1) 71–74.

turn he is overwhelmed. He cannot manage the interaction he so clearly longed for, so he retreats into a repetitive behaviour that his brain recognises, tapping his lip with a piece of jigsaw. At least now, in the middle of chaos, his brain has somewhere it can anchor. Focusing on this sensation David knows what he is doing.

In order to capture David's attention I have to try and work out an alternative approach, although as with John, this is more a matter of trial and error than decision. The first is visual mirroring: I do what he is doing and tap my lip. But, just as the feedback John was giving himself was auditory, so the way David is talking to himself is through proprioception. I am making a mistake if I think that because he is tapping himself, he will automatically recognise that I am doing the same. In this case, direct mirroring is not effective. It is the tapping that David is interested in. He does not 'see' my copying. The whole point of David's tapping is to switch off the surplus sensory intake, so that he is hanging on to at least something that makes sense.

So I need to use the same stimulatory route that he is using to calm himself – proprioception – and in this case I opt for vibration. Rather than approaching the area of his face where he is tapping directly, I get his teacher to place the vibration unit on the back of the chair he is leaning his head on and, since he does not reject this, gradually move it towards his cheek. In a minute or so he realises that he is receiving a recognisable and contingent stimulus, but one that is even more powerful than he is giving himself. He takes note of this, grabs the vibration unit, applies it to his mouth, ear and jaw, and lifts his head with a delighted smile. As he searches for the source of the stimulus he is no longer locked into himself but looks at us. David is sharing an experience that clearly has meaning for him.

Sometimes we have to take a roundabout route to interaction. Consider Beryl: she is in her 20s and has severe autism. She does not connect with people and spends much of her time in a very disturbed state. When she is particularly upset her care staff take her for a walk and she calms down. Beryl is not happy with my presence and does not respond to my attempts to engage with her through her sounds so we decide to take her out. We start off walking along the busy road outside her house. It has a very narrow pavement so I am forced to walk behind her. She smacks her feet onto the rather hollow and echoing paving stones in a very noisy way, so I smack my feet on the ground in the same rhythm as hers. While Beryl gives no overt sign that my action is significant to her, there is something about our synchrony that gives me a feeling that she has recognised my response to the stimulus she is giving herself and is beginning to take notice. After a while, I deliberately place my foot down quietly, withholding 'her sound', so that the feedback that I am giving her is discontinuous, pulling the rug on her expectation. She stops at once, spins round and looks at me, laughing. Our relationship changes as we share the joke.

## The dopamine reward

Recognition is defined as, 'knowing again', 'recalling to mind', or more concurrently, 'been there, done that, got the T-shirt'. It is embedded, with the implication that the behaviour or object that is recognised is something the brain has previously witnessed and recorded. We now know that in our bodies this 'familiarity' is flagged up by the rewarding squirt of the neurotransmitter dopamine – the feel-good factor.

However, one of the more surprising outcomes of using body language to communicate is that imitation and its modifications appear to be more effective in establishing attention when it is not simple mimicry that is used, but rather a similar approach that contains an additional element of something unusual, framed in the familiar. It is not just that the brain gets used to a stimulus and learns to ignore it as being of no significance (habituation). As mentioned in the previous chapter, an act of recognition that also involves an element of surprise, gives us four times the pleasurable reinforcement of dopamine than that which stems from a simple mimicry recognition on its own.[79] The consequence of this is that the brain is programmed to look for new experiences, particularly those that we recognise as building on our existing repertoire. As we shall see, this positive response to surprise is important: imitation in itself will get attention but using a partner's body language in a surprising context shifts the brain from attention to engagement. Our partners want to explore this new manifestation of 'their' stimuli.

---

79   Lehrer J (2009) *The Decisive Moment*. Edinburgh: Canongate Books.

When we first meet, the effort of processing all the new stimuli presented by a stranger throws Beryl into a state of sensory overload. She attacks herself and others, trying to communicate her distress and reduce her confusion by generating a pattern of behaviour that will result in her being taken for a walk, so that she can listen to the rhythmic slap-slap of her noisy footfall. It may sound simple, but when she hears and can focus on this in the midst of her sensory chaos, it reduces the painful turmoil in her head to the point at which she knows what she is doing.

So I tune in to the pattern of sound that Beryl recognises. Her brain is drawn to this: 'This is part of my vital pattern I recognise but I did not initiate it.' She shifts her attention to the source outside herself and listens. As she becomes more certain that her rhythm and mine are linked, her brain builds up an expectation – she is waiting for my next confirmation. So sure is she of this now that when I deliberately withhold my response she swings round laughing, acknowledging the game we were playing. Her attention is no longer on her distress but on our interaction.

# The infant-mother paradigm

The idea of working with non-verbal people's body language to get in touch with them was introduced by the psychologist Geraint Ephraim. Casting about for some way of tuning in to the people who he was asked to help, he had to acknowledge that his psychology degree was not offering him any way to reach them. One day, out of desperation, he started to copy the movements of a disturbed man with autism and was surprised when the man started to sit up and take notice. Ephraim tried this tactic with other people, both those with autism and people with severe learning disabilities, with similar positive responses. Once he joined in with what his partner was doing, the two of them seemed to slide into a conversation, similar to the one that characterises the infant-mother relationship. (When the baby makes a movement or sound, the mother confirms its initiative, liberating the baby to move on to try out something else. Put simply, the baby says 'boo', the mother responds 'boo' and after a little while playing around with this the baby tries out something else.) This process is so intimate that the observer feels excluded. Mother and infant appear to be totally locked into each other in mutual fascination, through attention, gaze and response. If all is going well with the relationship this is a game that mothers fall into naturally. Called dyadic behaviour, it is fundamental to the growth of attachment and underlies the infant's capacity both to communicate and to develop emotional engagement.[80]

# Before birth

However, thanks to technology intimacy can now start before birth. Blurry photographs introduce parent and infant in the womb and make sense of the startling independent lumps that elbow the walls of the belly. This trampolining embryo is real, already imprinting its individuality, an independent 'not me' inside 'me'. Through scanners I can see it sucking its thumb, exercising *in utero*, swimming around and turning somersaults. The baby arrives fully primed for communication. Although it was previously supposed that it took weeks after birth for the baby to develop the capacity to copy, it has now been shown that at 20 minutes old, when the mother sticks out her tongue the infant copies her.[81] Imitation works for both partners and continues to be attractive throughout our lives.

So what is going on in the brain when it re-experiences something it has met before?

# Macaque monkeys and mirror neurons

Since the 1980s it has been clear to practitioners who use 'imitation' of body language to communicate with people on the autistic spectrum that this simple approach is an effective way of getting close to people, provided that the responses we use are linked

---

80  The dyad is the term used to express the exclusive and intimate connection between mother and infant while they are communicating through body language. Zeedyk observes that they are so wrapped up in each other that to the outsider it looks as though one is seeing them inside a glass bubble. (Private group seminar.)

81  Nagy E (2006) From imitation to conversation: the first dialogues with human neonates. *Infant and Child Development* **15** 223–232.

or closely related to the patterns of behaviour that their brain is already familiar with. However, it is only recently that we are starting to learn why this is. As so often happens in scientific investigation, the really interesting breakthroughs emerge when the unexpected happens and instead of ignoring the 'awkward' result, the researcher takes note and uses the anomaly as a springboard to look at the problem they have in a different way: 'Why doesn't this work the way I think it should? Maybe I need to modify my hypothesis.'

The story starts in Italy, with macaque monkeys and peanuts. Giacomo Rizzolatti and his colleagues are studying what happens in neurobiological terms when the hand makes a particular movement – in this case, when the monkey picks up a peanut and eats it.[82]

Coincident with its hand movement, the brain responds by firing specific neurons. What is both fascinating and unanticipated is that when the monkey sees the hungry experimenter idly pick up a nut and put it in his mouth, the same sensory pattern fires off in the monkey's brain as would have done if the monkey had made the identical movement itself. Work with modern scanners confirms that humans also possess this network of nerve cells that are now called mirror neurons.[83, 84]

# Feeling your feeling

When I see you doing an action that I recognise, not only are you feeling it at the time, but I also feel it in me and respond to what I see you doing. The commonest example, one that we are all familiar with, is that when I see you yawn, the chances are that I will start yawning, or at least feel a pre-yawn tickle in my jaw muscles. Neurons fire off the motor pattern in your brain that triggers your yawn and when I see you open your mouth an identical motor pattern fires off in my brain, causing me to yawn too.

---

82 Rizzolatti G, Fadiga L, Gallese V & Fogassi L (1996) Premotor cortex and the recognition of motor actions. *Cognitive Brain Research* **3** 131–141.
83 Gallese V, Fadiga L, Fogassi L & Rizzolatti G (1996) Action recognition in the premotor cortex. *Brain* **119** (2) 593–609.
84 Iacobini M, Woods R, Brass M, Bekkering H, Mazziota JC & Rizzolatti G (1999) Cortical mechanisms of human imitation. *Science* **286** 2526–2528.

Here is another example: A man has come to mend my computer. I offer him coffee but do not have one myself since I have just finished one. As we are talking he stretches out his hand and lifts his cup. Without thinking, I find myself reaching out to the table to raise my non-existent cup to my lips. His action has triggered off a motor pattern in my muscles that leads me to copy his movement. I can actually feel his movement in my arm.

Or I see a small boy launching himself from a top step into his mother's arms. She catches him and he is so pleased that he frog-hops all the way to the shop. Walking behind him, I am surprised to feel the motor signals of his leaps in my hips and thighs and catch myself making an experimental jump, (mirror neurons capturing his action and sending out motor signals). He catches my movement out of the corner of his eye and turns, laughing, rubbing his hands with glee.

This works for hearing as well. A macaque mirror neuron that fires when the monkey rips paper, also fires when it hears (but does not see) someone else rip paper. Newborn baby macaques are even able to copy human facial expressions, sticking out their tongues when a human sticks out theirs. Here lies the real mystery. Since the baby (macaque or human) has never seen its mother's – or any other – tongue before, how does it know what its own tongue is, that the thing that it can only feel is the same as what it sees outside of itself? How does it translate this new experience into a sensory motor pattern that allows it to copy what it sees?

To ask such a question presupposes that my brain is storing up memories in the form of flashcards through which it rifles in search of a match, when in fact what I see – my visual intake – is transmitted to the brain not in the form of images but as electrical impulses travelling along the membranes of nerve cells. It is in this form that incoming messages from the world outside are compared with patterns of stored information. Looked at in this light we get a different picture. Through ultrasound explorations we learn that babies in the womb are already opening and closing their mouths, drinking up to a pint of amniotic fluid a day, and drawing on their thumbs. In preparation for the need to attach themselves to their mother's nipple they are practising rooting and sucking, already exercising the muscles of the cheeks and tongue.[85] Is this the near-enough pattern that enables them to recognise and copy their mother's initiative?

As a baby, I come into this world pretty well prepared, sentient, with a survival imperative written into my script – the need to recognise what is going on and the ability to react accordingly. I am tuned into imitation games from the beginning, primed to copy you, and when I smile, you will copy me. In this way I learn to marry the different senses. I see you stick out your tongue, match the image to a motor pattern that is already part of my sensory motor repertoire ('I recognise this trick, I was doing it at around six months in the womb'), and feel my tongue stick out. What I see is the same as what I feel.

However, as we have already seen in discussion of the dopamine reward, the patterns don't need to be an exact match. Daniel Stern cites the case of Eric, a passive infant whose mother engages with him only when he shows an interest in her.

> *'She encourages, even intensifies the experience so that he enjoys a higher level of excitement than he would on his own. Her cajoling, exaggerating, slightly over-responsive eliciting behaviour are very enjoyable to Eric ... and does not cause a gross mismatch but rather a small one. His tolerance for stimulation can encompass it ... as she tries to augment the range of his experiences.'* [86]

Tapping into the most powerful biological directive that we have (and one that stays with us throughout our lives, even, as we are now learning, into senility), the basic urge to communicate allows us to reach people who are otherwise totally isolated from human contact.

Nevertheless, getting it right involves many processes which have to synchronise and on occasion we find that in spite of our best efforts we are misjudging the sensory scenario. Daniel Stern points out that:

---

85  Tallack P (2006) *In the Womb*. Washington DC: National Geographic Society.
86  Stern D (1985) *The Interpersonal World of the Infant*. New York: Basic Books.

> '...the capacity to transfer information from one modality to another is so central to integrating perceptual experience that the potential problems resulting from a deficit are almost limitless'.[87]

# Disorientation

We all, autistic or not, very quickly become disorientated and disturbed by discrepancies between expectation and experience, or a lack of sensory signposts. To know how this feels, try walking through the Imperial War Museum in Manchester, where the walls are deliberately constructed off-true, as though they had been hastily assembled from some bombed-out shards. Our eyes tell us that this is something different to what we expect from walls, which our experience tells us should be vertical. The first thing we do is put out our hands to check (through touch) our distorted visual experience. Visitors to Antony Gormley's Blind Light exhibition experienced a similar disquiet as they groped their way through a light-filled vapour cloud.[88] From outside, they can be seen spreading their hands on the glass walls, checking on orientation, seeking and keeping in touch with their sense of self through haptic sensation.

If we don't receive the correct signals or we cannot process them properly, we need to be able to cross-reference quickly from one sense to another in order to extract ourselves. We are constantly checking up on ourselves, looking for confirmation both from our surroundings and from people, just as we did on our mother's knee. It is this feedback that tells us that we are, that we exist.

In a psychological sense, if we look for feedback from people and get none, we feel uncertain on a scale that varies from feeling mildly rejected (for example, when trying to engage with an autistic partner whose apparent awareness of our existence extends no further than treating us like a lump of wood), to feeling totally isolated, which is in biological terms very threatening – we shall have no allies who will help us to protect ourselves when needs be. Just as when I was stuck in the lift, under these circumstances

---

[87] Stern D (1985) *The Interpersonal World of the Infant*. New York: Basic Books.
[88] Gormley A (2007) Blind Light. Art exhibition. London: Hayward Gallery, August 2007.

I look for physical feedback that I can focus on. But what if both human and physical feedback overload me and feel threatening, as is the case for many people on the autistic spectrum? Then I shall have to narrow down my point of focus to a single reliable repetitive stimulus from which I can retain at least some sense of who and what I am.

## Using a kazoo

I am trying to engage the attention of a young child, Linda, but her gaze is abstracted; she seems to be on autopilot, as if in another world. She plays with toys that make sounds, a merry-go-round with swinging bells, a bar with hanging bells and another merry-go-round with wooden pegs that clack against each other. In spite of her evident interest in sound, she seems deaf to the human voice in the sense that when I or others speak to her, there is no light in her eyes, she does not turn towards me or make any appropriate response. If it wasn't for her interest in toys that make noises one might assume that she is deaf. However, it is not that she can't hear, rather that there is something about interaction with people and 'people sound' that she is unable to cope with. I decide to see what will happen if I use a kazoo to answer the sounds that she makes.

The result is immediate and electrifying, quite unlike any previous response. She turns round with a radiant smile and holds out her hands to me, switched on and eager. I continue to answer her sounds for a short while but then she is overcome again and retreats to the corner where she places her hands over her ears. It is clear that in my pleasure at her response I have over-stimulated her, exceeding her capacity to cope.

It is a very fine line between under and overstimulation. Getting the level correct can be extremely tricky because the point of balance can shift without apparent warning. To return to Daniel Stern, talking about the development of children who are not on the spectrum, he says that:

> 'A point is reached when the infant's capacity to cope with the stimulation level is about to be exceeded. At this point

> *the child must down-regulate the level by dampening or terminating stimulus input through some coping manoeuvre, or the threshold for coping will be exceeded and the infant will experience something like panic.'*[89]

With people on the autistic spectrum we are often dealing with a sliding fulcrum: a sensory input that is tolerable and even pleasurable on one occasion may at another time be overtaken by a brain that interprets the input as a threat, with the consequent fear of tipping into the autonomic storm. The child needs to get out of the situation and withdraws, freezes or lashes out. However, in my work with Linda and the kazoo, before dismissing my overtures with the kazoo as an unworkable approach we need to try and understand what has happened. There are various possibilities.

The first is that I subjected her to over-the-top sound, which was more than she could cope with, although her initial response suggests that she was delighted with what she was hearing. Possibly there was too much visual stimulation as I moved closer to her, although I was still some way off. What seems more likely is that she was hypersensitive to her own internal response to her joy – the surge engendered by her trigger-happy autonomic nervous system – and she experienced what Donna Williams calls, 'emotional overload'.

This interpretation is in line with suggestions that (some) children with autism may have an extremely low tolerance for human stimulation but not for non-human stimulation.[90] I initially played the kazoo in response to Linda's sounds when she was standing with her back to me. It has an instrumental timbre rather than a human one. She turned towards me in answer to a response to her sound which felt safe but when she saw me it was too much to process. Hypersensitivity to one's own emotions is described as feeling like being drowned in a tidal wave of sensation. Linda put her fingers in her ears and walked resolutely to the door and exit.

So can we find a way of using this approach that puts the stimulus that Linda enjoys within a context that renders it safe – one that is

---

89 Stern D (1985) *The Interpersonal World of the Infant.* New York: Basic Books.
90 Hutt C & Ounsted C (1966) The biological significance of gaze aversion with particular reference to infantile autism. *Behavioural Science* **11** 346–356.

sufficiently limited to offer the connection that moved her without triggering her withdrawal? Possible lines of exploration relate to another response of hers: when I had engaged her attention by sharing in play with her bells, she climbed on my lap and dug her fingers into my back. Here she felt safe as she cuddled in.

# Failure of the mirror neuron system as a cause of autism

Taken together, the infant-mother paradigm and the mirror neuron theory combine to give us a very attractive hypothesis as to why Intensive Interaction is such an effective tool, particularly when used with people on the autistic spectrum. However, based on the difficulties they are alleged to have with copying movements, there is a school of thought that suggests that one of the deficits of the autistic brain is that the mirror neuron system is not working.[91]

However, in a review exposing weaknesses in the experimental methodology of research with humans (as opposed to monkeys), Dinstein and his colleagues suggest that it is unlikely that mirror neuron deficit is related to autism.[92] This is in line with the experience of practitioners using body language with their autistic partners. Once triggers to hypersensitive reactions are minimised and signals the brain is able to understand without elaborate processing are introduced, both children and adults on the spectrum are not only able to copy but also to take part in a two-way 'conversation', whereby they will take it in turns to copy or initiate, as in any dialogue. A reasonable analogy of the autistic failure to be able to copy under so-called 'normal' conditions, is suggested by the experience of a deaf person who, while able to hear in a quiet space, is unable to pick out words against the background noise in a busy room. Similarly, a woman with autism confirms that she is able to enjoy the film *Transformers* when the room is empty, but if it fills up with people she gets overloaded and sensorily distressed.[93] As contrasted with hearing impairment,

91  Ramachandran VS (2011) *The Tell-tale Brain*. London: William Heinemann, p137.
92  Dinstein I, Thomas C, Behrmann M & Heeger DJ (2008) A mirror up to nature. *Current Biology* **18** (1) 13–18.
93  WeirdGirlCyndi (2007) *Sensory Overload Simulation* [online]. Available at: http://www.youtube.com/watch?v=BPDTEuotHe0 (accessed February 2012).

in the case of autism the background 'business' originates within the brain rather than from outside.

## Can people with autism copy?

A child with extreme autism, who is totally unable to cope in a noisy classroom, is able to interact with his teacher through body language in a quiet area. He is making a necklace, piece by piece. His teacher copies him, making her own. He starts to look at hers and next copies what she does, putting in extra pieces where she has them on hers. He then leans over and adjusts hers. Finally he takes off on his own; rooting in his box of pieces he comes up with some more and, while they are still both wearing their necklaces, joins the two of them together. Unable to speak, he has found a way of expressing their intimacy in his own language. When she tells me, his teacher is in tears.

It appears that the network of mirror neurons works not only for actions but also for feelings. Place two people under scanners and show one a picture of a face registering disgust and the same pattern fires off in them and in the brain of the observer. This allows us to speculate on our own intuitive recognition of our partner's feelings, especially when these are non-verbal. One way or another we are picking up subliminal emotional signals from our partners, seeming to employ a kind of affective satellite navigation system that – if we learn to pay attention to its prompts – tells us whereabouts our conversation partner is on the scale of feeling. It is easy to pick up feelings such as depression for example. But more subtly, in between the extremes of joy and despair, once we begin to pay attention to the motor prompts of our own 'mind-map', we become extremely sensitive to minute changes in our partner's affect. To say, 'This is my perception of how my partner feels,' is more than just interpretation; it seems to be a genuine response in my brain through my mirror neuron system to my partner's affective state. Something has altered between us and refocuses my attention, as though someone had tweaked a string between our brains. This is where I need to pay total attention. As well as observing what my partner is doing I must listen simultaneously to the subliminal nudges offered by my mirror neuron system, so that

I can fine-tune in to how my partner feels. I do this by focusing in on their body language, all the sounds and movements they make, and especially the affective quality of their initiatives. How does what they are doing feel in me?

## The second person response: 'insidesight'

Remembering Vasu Reddy's suggestion that when we attend to each other we evoke a second-person response, she suggests that in a dyadic situation we are not just separate observers, nor are we extensions of each other by projection; we are interpersonally linked. I am affected by what you do and this shapes my response so that we are already both part of our interaction in a very personal way.[94]

Put simply, if body language is the voice of affect, then communication is not just the words you speak or the way you look at me, but rather what I hear you say and how I interpret your look and vice versa. Putting aside for the minute insight into my own behaviour, insight into how you feel implies that I am looking at 'you in there' from an external position. I should prefer to call this capacity 'insidesight' – 'you reflected in me', since my perception of you is at least partly derived internally through the agency of my mirror neurons. Your action, my motor message derived from your action and my response to this are part of each other.

---

94  Reddy V (2008) *How Infants Know Minds*. Cambridge, MA: Harvard University Press.

# Chapter 6

# Talking to myself

## Giving value to the way people feel

If we look at two people engaged in Intensive Interaction, one of whom is autistic and one who is not on the spectrum, we notice that they are psychologically enfolded in each other; their focus is totally engaged in their partner. Although we may be witnessing an interaction between adults, the feel of what we see bears some relationship to the mother-infant dyadic relationship but at the same time with the characteristics of a more equal partnership. In such an interaction it does not feel as if I am 'mothering' but rather being led by an open-ended and respectful curiosity to explore what my partner has to offer, while offering them sensory inputs presented in such a way that they both have meaning for them and demonstrate my empathy for whatever they are feeling – an affective interest that puts me alongside their joy or distress.

There is a sense in which I am totally unaware of my partner's autism, or any other disability they may have (although this is qualified by a sensitivity to any moves I might make that could increase their stress level). What is pre-eminent in this second-person relationship is the incredible privilege of being allowed access to another mind and the flow between us. It is not that I am the giver and my partner is the taker, rather that whatever is shared between us is given and received in equal measure. The interaction is important, rather than the separate acts. Totally inseparable and responsive, we are engaged in an intimacy that excludes our surroundings. However long or brief our encounter, the game we are playing is deadly serious.

In the middle of a filmed intervention, my partner apparently breaks off and darts forward to pick a piece of fluff off of my jersey. When they see this apparent interruption the audience almost always laughs. But what is important to my partner, and therefore to me, is her urgency (how she feels), which I feel in me and respond to in kind. She glances up and our eyes meet. We have now an understanding of what her compulsion means to her. Nothing exists but our relationship, an exchange that is about respect for everything that my partner is, and about listening to what my partner is telling me about how she feels, not just through words but also through her body language.

I make no judgment about the following story, except that it illustrates how urgent it is that we hear what people are telling us – in this case a child.

It happens that as I come out of a respite home with a student, two small boys are standing in the drive with their bikes, peering in fascination into the window at a resident who is bellowing. One says rather belligerently, 'What's he doing?' I reply that he is unhappy. The boy says, 'Why's he unhappy?' Slightly at a loss, I hear myself answer, 'Because his brain is not wired up properly'. Unexpectedly my questioner says very quietly, 'My brain's not wired up properly'. His voice is that of a sad child. At this point one of the support workers comes out and shouts at the children, telling them they are bad boys: 'I know your mother and you're a bad lot! I'll come after you.' Immediately that child mutates into a screaming vandal, running his bike at her and spitting.

In theory, and for the sake of privacy, I and the student who was with me should have asked the children to leave at once but instead we were somehow drawn into an exchange that was deeply poignant. The interruption, like a severe jolt to the psyche, was shocking. On the edge of a really important conversation, we received the impression that no one had listened to what the boy felt before. We have to be so careful not to steamroller authentic feelings, which in some respect are our most precious possessions since they define for us who we are.

A man on the autistic spectrum is extremely volatile. He spends his days in his room or, if he comes out, he roams around rearranging furniture. When I arrived I was warned that he was on the edge of an outburst. In order to avoid adding to his sensory overload, I sat with a student outside his room and gently answered his sounds. After a while he came out and sat with us. He wriggled his foot, so we wriggled ours back. Gradually he moved from agitation to calm; he was so calm that his support staff remarked they had never seen him like that before. At this juncture a cheerful woman burst through the doors and, unaware of our intervention, shouted at him that he looked silly in his paper hat. Something extremely precious shattered in the life of a man who is deeply disturbed – the spell was broken and he returned to his restless patrolling.

We can only help each other if we are not only sensitive to but also show that we give value to each other's feelings.

Within the dyadic relationship, the stream of affect has tangible qualities. Sometimes it is as if one is handling lengths of fine silk that unwrap light trapped in their sheen. For those who are strangers to the value of using body language, they are most likely to have come across this feeling when quietly with a lover, not doing anything but just being with them so that, through intimate attention, they are totally aware of every minute change in mood. It is as if the pair are joined by a cord, but unlike the navel cord, feeding is two-way.

But if such closeness is directly contrary to even the name of autism (a word deliberately chosen to express the isolation experienced by those on the spectrum), what is happening when we experience this closeness and how can it happen? How do we move from isolation to mutual attention or, as Josh would describe it, 'delicious conversation'?[95]

# Sensory disorientation and fear

Before trying to move from autistic isolation to mutual intimate attention, we need to consider in more detail, the nature and origins of sensory disorientation. It is now clear that confusion and fear

---
95   Harris J (2012) *Joshua's Planet* [online]. Available at: www.joshuasplanet.com (accessed May 2012).

are caused by failure to accurately process the signals from the outside world received by the ears, the skin and the eyes. Take vision: visual processing is not a straightforward single process but involves many different minor processes, any of which can be out of sync with the others and so throw the whole system out of order. Or vision may cross over with sound, so that there is an auditory outcome from a visual intake, as in the condition known as synaesthesia. Bizarre as it may seem to the outsider, any of our senses may be cross-referencing, for example, particular tastes being realised as shapes. Then there are also tangled signals from the inner sensors of muscular movement and messages from the nervous system (those which cause emotional overload). Synaesthesia, which is not confined to people on the autistic spectrum, is as if a playful kitten had been let loose in our neural processing skeins.

## Off-balance

Adding to the confusion, there is the sense that we tend to overlook: the vestibulocochlear (balance) system. This is the one that we take for granted: three looped canals inside the ear, one sensing on each plane – upwards, sideways and backwards and forwards – as we move. Fluid swills over sensitive cells sending messages to the brain, telling us which direction we are moving in, orientating us in our environment. But this secret labyrinth is also interconnected with sensory processing and functional outcomes, and involved in our perception of time and movement.[96] For example, when we hear a sound it is the vestibular system that locates the direction that it is coming from. If we move our heads it stabilises our gaze and this stability is critical. 'It is the reference point from which all sensation is organised.'[97] It is not difficult to imagine that at least some of the zooming and swirling visual effects described by people with autism who are diagnosed as having scotopic sensitivity, may relate to problems with the balance organ.

Looking through an estate agent window at a display of house photographs, I do not realise that the board is being adjusted from

---

96  Frick SM & Hacker C (2001) *Listening with the Whole Body*. Madison, WI: Vital Links.
97  Ayres AJ (1979) *Sensory Integration and the Child*. Los Angeles, CA: Western Psychological Services.

the behind. When it starts to swing, I am momentarily caught off balance – I feel as though I am swinging and the board is stationary. The unrecognised movement sets up conflict with my notion of my own stability. I do not know what is happening and start to sway. Beyond mild disturbances such as this, damage to the balance organ can have catastrophic effects. In his book on neuroplasticity, *The Brain that Changes Itself*, Norman Doidge introduces us to a woman whose vestibular system, as a side-effect of a drug, has failed completely and gives her no feedback at all.

She wobbles, feeling as if she is made of jelly. She has to hold on to a wall to walk. She always feels like she is falling, even when she has already fallen. As well as this disorientation, she tells us of:

> *'the constant mental fatigue. It takes brain power simply to maintain a vertical position – brain power that is taken away from such mental functions as memory and the ability to calculate and reason.'* [98]

# Failure to wire up correctly

When the brain fails to 'wire up' properly due to disrupted neural connections, the situation arises that leads to the sensory chaos so characteristic of autism.[99] One might visualise a faulty satellite navigation system that constantly directs the user the wrong way round one-way systems and into cul-de-sacs. In discussions on neuroplasticity, Doidge suggests that the brain can be trained to rewire itself but admits that in order to accomplish this it is essential to have attention[100] – difficult to attain if one is on the run from devastating sensory overload. In order to immerse the brain in a setting favourable to development, one must use familiar and non-threatening material. Temple Grandin suggests that if one wishes to teach a child to read and they love aeroplanes, then one must stick the letters and words on the side of pictures of aeroplanes. The message has to be delivered in such a way that it does not trigger the body's self-defence system (force-feeding will

---

98  Doidge N (2007) *The Brain that Changes Itself*. London: Penguin Books, p5.
99  Morrow EM et al (2008) Identifying autism loci and genes by tracing recent shared ancestry. *Science* **321** (5886) 218–223.
100 Doidge *op.cit*.

heighten the stress levels). All this turbulence is overshadowed by fear of being overwhelmed by the autonomic storm when 'all the fuses blow'.[101] In the face of sensory overload and without a point of reference to hold on to, our partners are lost.

Occasionally it seems that total immersion from a very early age can help to rewire an autistic child's brain that is badly disorientated. Mukhopadhyay's mother simply did not believe that her son could not be rescued and she talked to him non-stop from his early childhood. Amazingly she was able to draw him out from his chaotic perception.[102] This probably depends on the level of ability of the child and one cannot tell how disabled a child is until their sensory difficulties have been reduced.

# Self-regulation

However severe the disability, the brain is a fighter and constantly tries to make sense of what is happening. Organisation is what so many people with autism are aiming for. In an effort to maintain at least some intelligible order in an environment that manifests with all the instability of a wobble board, is there something that our partners can do that allows them to know what they are doing? Many people will focus on tapping or some such obvious physical activity, but some of their references are more subtle.

Here is a man with severe autism who smokes. He seems to do so, not so much to inhale but rather to watch the blue veils of smoke swirl up from his cigarette (or from the candle in his aromatherapy session). The thin seductive spiral fines down to extinction, to the fascinating place where 'is' becomes 'is not'. Total attention stills his mind.

# Harnessing points of reference

When we are looking for ways to get in touch with our partners, such points of reference help to anchor the brain and guide them

---

101 Williams D (1998) *Somebody Somewhere: Breaking free from the world of autism*. London: Jessica Kingsley Publishers.

102 Mukhopadhyay TR (2008) *How Can I Talk if My Lips Don't Move? Inside my autistic mind*. New York: Arcade Publishing.

through the sensory jungle. Take a child with Asperger's syndrome. She loves horses and is completely incontinent, unable to go to the toilet because she is terrified of the sound of the cistern flushing. The sucking sound overwhelms her and literally hurts. She is genuinely afraid. Her aunt resolves the problem by sticking a picture of a horse on the tank. Her niece's interest in the picture overrides her fear: concentrating on the horse enables her to stem the tide of panic that threatens to engulf her.

# Compulsion

Before we write off such behaviours as obsessional, we must remember that most are extensions of our own behaviours. They are, from the point of view of the person whose brain is spinning like an agitated kaleidoscope, self-preservatory attempts to keep the brain on track, so that those caught up in the turmoil can at least in one sense predict the consequences of what that they are doing. Those of us who support people with autism need to be aware that the effect of trying to limit such defensive strategies is to remove any hope of self-regulation, leaving our partner totally vulnerable to the often painful sensations that their brain can no longer process. If compliance is achieved, it is at the cost of increased anxiety and stress, and payment is frequently made in raised levels of aggression. To try and control self-stimulation directly is like snatching the lifebelt from a drowning man – life-threatening with all of its neurobiological consequences. What we need to explore is how we, the outsider, can turn this around so that the maintenance of reality for our partners becomes part of exchange and their attention is redirected into 'other' rather than locked (for protection) into 'self'. Is it possible to arrange a mutual environment that provides the life-saving stability characteristic of a fixation but is at the same time interactive? What advantages if any does this have?

# The delicious conversation

Returning to Josh (who we met in Chapter 1), he chooses his words with care. Unable to speak, when he is typing he has nevertheless been known to select a Hebrew word if it is more apposite than an English one. So why choose the word 'delicious' to describe his wordless interactions with his companions? A word that suggests not only pleasure but like 'delightful' implies concurrent attention to the source of his pleasure: 'I am enjoying this, not just retrospectively but now while it is happening.' His focus is on the present exchange.

'Delicious' is a word rooted in sensory pleasure: in this case, 'highly pleasant to the taste', according to the *Oxford Dictionary of English*.[103] Unlike more general adjectives such as 'nice', 'pleasant' (and in my part of the world, the expansive 'grand'), 'delicious' is very specific. It points like the unerring needle of a compass to the present position, having the curious quality of rescuing flavour from the past and anticipating it from the future – shifting it (forwards or backwards) from 'then' to 'now'. It draws attention from 'other time' to here. Chocoholics think 'chocolate' and salivate in contingent desire.

To attribute 'delicious' to a conversation implies that it is not just special but especially special. With our senses highly attentive, we are 'all eyes', 'all ears', even our skin is on 'red alert'. So what is it that makes this affective conversation so precious that it harnesses all our attention?

# Faulty processing

One reason is simple: security. Being a human being is an uncertain business. To adapt to this the brain has evolved an elaborate system of sensors in an early warning system designed to protect the body from injury. Signals received from the outside world are decoded and sorted into those that are user-friendly and those that represent potential danger. On the one hand we look for allies to support us, and on the other, hostile signals are fast-tracked to the part of the brain that deals with emergencies (either real or perceived as real) so that appropriate action can be set in motion. Whether or not this is a response to a real threat depends on an accurate interpretation of the stream of information being received from the senses. At the first intimation of danger a cascade process is triggered by the hypothalamus, which sends corticotrophin-

103 *Oxford Dictionary of English* (2nd ed) (2003) Oxford: Oxford University Press.

releasing hormone to the pituitary gland. This in turn activates the adrenal gland, pumping the stress hormones cortisol and adrenalin into the blood stream, preparing the body for a defensive response. As we have already seen, the problem for people on the autistic spectrum is that while their sense organs may be functioning normally, by the time the inputs have attempted the perilous voyage through the processing system, the overall picture of what is going on around our partners is hopelessly scrambled.

# Hypersensitivity

Much of what the non-autistic person interprets as benign or even pleasurable (such as a smile or praise) can be interpreted by someone with autism as negative, even to the point of triggering the body's self-defence system with consequent protective reactions. Hormones alert me to a state of terror, so I am going to run, freeze or lash out. While we know in general that the trouble lies in a processing system that easily gets out of sync with the rate of incoming stimuli, exactly what it is that underlies such a failure in any one person is difficult to untangle. Different people feel threatened by different triggers. Hypersensitivities to external stimuli may mean that signals, for example bright light, can be misconstrued as (potentially) threatening and an unreliable autonomic nervous system translates this into a warning signal – pain. Alternatively, objects may be only partially perceived – in bits, or distorted – wriggling bits instead of a whole. Processing may also be made more difficult by certain colours. 'In-your-face' patterns can throw the system completely.[104]

In an effort to hold back the chaos, the brain may fixate on one object in the room and see absolutely nothing else at all. A small boy knows that if he needs to go to the lavatory, he should place his knee near a bunch of flowers – the posy in question being a stencil on the back of the toilet seat. He does not see the toilet itself, the bath, the door and the medicine cabinet. His whole attention is focused on the one thing that has meaning for him. This is where he can pee.

---

104 This hypersensitivity to light and consequent visual distortion is called Irlen syndrome or scotopic sensitivity. It does not show up in a normal eye test and requires a colorometric test. The colour of the lenses required is specific to the individual.

It is extremely difficult for a non-autistic person to realise just what is meant by hypersensitivity. We tend to think of it as a (perhaps) uncomfortable extension of our own sensory experience. How can we consolidate this with a woman with autism's description of the sound of a falling snowflake being like glass shattering?[105] This is an auditory experience? It is completely beyond the range of what we know.

Visual disturbance can also be compounded by auditory booms and silences, and noises in certain frequencies that are acutely painful. The vestibular (balance) system weaves an erratic path. While the tactile system may be oversensitive to touch, our partner is very often hyposensitive (under-sensitive) to proprioception – the internal sensations from muscles, joints and nerves that tell us where we are in space and what we are doing. For example, standing on our toes helps us to experience what proprioception feels like with pressures and strains fed back to the brain by sensors in the calves, ankles and knees.

Particular confusion is rooted in the difficulties encountered in processing the spoken word. Some partners on the spectrum are unable to make sense of anything that is said to them, while others like Josh can probably understand most of it when they are not being overloaded by other sensory inputs like those outlined above. However, even if they are able to understand what is being said, people may still be unable to process replies, a situation that Therese Jolliffe describes as being so frustrating that she wants to 'scream and break things'.[106]

If you have autism, in order to get through to you without adding to your sensory distress, my head and heart need to work together, so I do not just sympathise through an effort of will but truly align myself with (and in) you. What I need to consider is how I can best navigate the minefield of your sensory dysfunction.

---

105 Personal communication with the author.
106 Jolliffe T, Lansdown R & Robinson C (1992) Autism: a personal account. *Communication* **26** (3) 12–19.

# The brain-body language

So what I am looking for is anything I can read in your body language that is helping you to make sense of your world, because it is precisely these familiar sensations that will form the basis of our mutual conversation. This is the language I shall use to infiltrate your world, keeping a lookout for what it is that your movements, gestures, rhythms and sounds, whatever they are, tell me about how you feel. Like any language, we shall become more skilled with practice.

Yet those of us who are non-verbal find it extremely difficult to make the switch over and abstain from using words. It is instinctive to talk. We want to establish some sort of relationship that tells us where we stand in the other person's regard. If they will not talk to us we feel in some way uncomfortable, diminished and rejected.

So what is it about this silence that we are afraid of? Does it leave us exposed to ballooning affect? Andrei Makine suggests that we talk in order to exorcise silence.[107] On the other hand, an old rabbi distinguishes between cognition and perception. He tells us: 'He did not like to talk, words are cruel, they play tricks … conceal the heart, the heart speaks in silence.'[108]

In some ways he is right. If we turn into and enter silence, we find the metaphorical heart can speak more powerfully than words, so much so that we can almost feel ourselves drowning in its stream. And yet, looked at through the eyes of reason, the heart is a two-up, two-down pump: frontman for a small walnut shaped organ in the brain called the amygdala. This is where the affective executive decisions are made. It is from here that the messages are sent out, dictating whether or not I shall feel fear or warmth. My beating heart, sweating skin and churning stomach simply reflect a process going on in my brain. If that is not enough, modern scanners suggest that empathy stems not so much from an effusion of the heart but from recognition by a collection of mirror neurons that fire off in my brain, in the same way that if I see that you are sad, the chances are that I will feel your sadness in myself. As we have already seen, it is not only actions but also feelings that can be caught.

---

107  Makine A (1995) *Le Testament Français*. London: Sceptre.
108  Potok C (1966) *The Chosen*. London: Penguin Group.

Yet we continue to ascribe our emotions to the organ that we call the heart: 'heartbroken' (desolate), 'heart in one's mouth/in one's boots' (fear and anticipation of fear), 'put your heart at rest' (be easy), 'after my own heart' (feel the same as me), 'lose one's heart to' (fall in love with), 'wear one's heart on one's sleeve', 'hand on heart', 'heart to heart', and so on. It is in this sense that the heart is the core of our emotions, the affective centre, where we feel that we feel from – from breaking terror to the warm spread of joy throughout our bodies.

# Inner listening

I may monitor my own heartbeat to keep in touch with how I am feeling but at the same time I must attend to the mind-map provided by my mirror neurons, in order to read how my partner's feeling feels in me. As we become more sensitive to the signals sent by our mirror neuron system we notice that there are times when we are aware of changes in our conversation partner that we do not consciously recognise at the time. For example, I am talking to a student about the times when a person with autism becomes so upset that their body's self-defence system is triggered and they become aggressive. In connection with this, I mention 'the autonomic nervous system'. There is no apparent change in my conversation partner's facial language, he does not say anything, but at the same time I am aware that he has not understood the term. Internally I notice what can only be described as a break in the link between us. It is as though I am watching the sweep of a second hand that suddenly jumps a few seconds. There is a hitch in the flow of non-verbal understanding between us and the continuity is broken.

I suspect that there must have been some subliminal hairline sensory tweak, which I did not pick up consciously but which nevertheless was recorded by my mirror neuron circuit. What I have to do is to learn to take notice of my inner message board so that each time I become even faintly aware of a discontinuity dragging its heels through ensuing interaction, I revisit it rather than dismiss it. In doing this I shall prop open the door between my consciousness and my semiconscious mirror neuron system and so become more sensitive to my partner's feelings. It is all a question of learning to pay attention to the momentary twitches in our own affective state, which tell us where we are in relation to our partner.

# Chapter 7

# A walk by the sea

## The predicting and modifying brain

I am walking through a museum passing rows of greyish-yellow bottled brains. Pickled, they look unattractive and inert – and certainly seem unrelated to the complex activity of an organ that is light-years removed from the phrenologist's models they resemble. The brain's 100 billion nerve cells and 500 trillion synaptic connections are in a constant state of flux, making predictions and modifying these in the light of what happens. The brain does this by strengthening or weakening the signals sent through adjacent neurons, constantly endeavouring to re-evaluate any erroneous forecasts, a catch-up, 'add-a-bit here' and 'take-a-bit there', system aimed at making sense of an uncertain world.[109] Everything the brain does is designed to minimise prediction error.[110] Unlike our domestic experience of electronic equipment, the repair man is constantly on hand, tinkering with the works, and making adjustments in wiring and firing to maximise effective response.

## Processing the emerging picture

What is clear is that to function successfully the brain is not only dependent on the sensory organs feeding in correct information from the outside world but also on accurate assessment of that information's potential. If variety is the spice of life, it is variation

---

109 Knill DC & Pouget A (2004) The Bayesian brain: the role of uncertainty in neural coding and computation for perception and action. *Trends in Neuroscience* **27** (12) 712–719.
110 Friston K & Stephan KE (2007) Free energy and the brain. *Synthese* **159** 417–458.

that keeps the system on its toes. Flexibility is critical. Even more important is the way that we assess, process and put the emerging picture into context. Can we use it to build up a working plan of the reality we experience, or is it plunging us into confusion?

# Paying attention

While it is relatively easy to pay attention to those activities that interest us, it is not always so easy to home in on things that do not immediately grab us and which demand effort. Either way, we must shift our attentional searchlight from our inner world to the world outside and beam in to whatever is going on around us. If we are to make anything of an object or activity, we have to attend to it with all of our senses. As it scans our horizons our periscope brain is searching for anything that looks interesting enough to stop it in its tracks, something that warrants investigation, to see if it offers a threat or advantage. Beyond its initial assessment the brain will withdraw, move on or engage as it sees fit. Identification is critical but also dependent on correct programming of the senses. If, as in the case of autism, all that the brain sees, feels and hears is threatening, then its responses will tend to be trigger-happy, jumping to the conclusion that all experience is hostile. Either way, the first priority is attention.

# Walking by the waves

We can learn a great deal about paying attention by watching waves, not necessarily crashing breakers that explode against jagged rocks in clouds of spume but on a day when the harr is down and an all-embracing sea mist wraps the seascape in a timeless cloak. There is no wind and the great swells running in from the Atlantic have shrunk to lazy tongues swiping the sand, a thin crease in the water's edge: an easy place to lose oneself in the reiterant whisper of the sea.

This Hebridean bay is shaped like a slice of melon. A rind of dunes backs an arc of lime-washed sand, derived entirely from white shells. Even though sky and water merge, the sea holds its pale green light like a bulb after the switch has been thrown, an emerald ember that continues to glow. Small flocks of dunlins worry the retreating edge of a silver tide for worms.

Attention is stilled to the waves, or rather to ripples because they are so shallow they barely turn down the edge. Each gathers in a different way, none quite the same as the one before, so that within the same parameters of water and sand, the senses are kept constantly on the hop. Today these leading edges are unusually dark, like an eyelid etched with kohl. The reason for this becomes clear when the ripples blink and break and spread themselves on the shore – the water is filled with thousands of tiny fragments of seaweed, bladders and thallus. Somewhere offshore the straps and thongs of kelp have been put through a storm shredder.

Hesitation. As the tide ebbs, the changing contours of the beach reshape the pattern: where will the break come this time? How far along will the suspended crest run? Just under the surface a rock tugs at the edges, swinging the line from oblique to circular eddies. Finally each lace curtain scrawls a unique signature on the sand, leaving behind a fringe of sifted grains so that, as the tide retreats it is possible to reconstruct the sequence of the ebb.

Gazing at the breaking waves, what holds our attention is the variation within a consistent framework. The busy cognitive brain is snagged on the 'will they/wont they' incipience of a hung wave that takes us right up to the wire. The eye that might otherwise habituate to duplication is constantly re-alerted to fresh combinations.

# Attention to self

Attention slides fairly easily into three categories: attention to self, attention to objects and attention to other people (reciprocated or unanswered as the latter case may be). To make the most of any of them requires lively curiosity and a desire to explore. There has to be some element in our encounter that makes us want to know what is going on, either in ourselves or around us.

Although as children we are constantly directed to pay attention to others, we also need to learn to pay attention to ourselves, not just to the feelings derived from our sensory impressions but also – since how we and our partners feel is the doorway to relationships – to the mind-maps that arise through interaction with others, as unless we learn to attend to these we shall never truly communicate. If we are to grow, we shall do so through the recognition of affective exchange in ourselves and in others; otherwise we are no better off than machines fed with data, simply becoming better machines but failing to increase our creative capacity.

In order to do this, we need to know how we feel, not just paying attention to the physical comforts and discomforts that arise from everyday encounters with reality but also to the messages from our inner world, the introspective shifts. We need to learn to be insightful into ourselves and how not to shy away from the tricky bits.

For my part, insight and introspection are night prowlers, padding through the territory of the semiconscious (what Claxton calls the 'undermind' [111]) in the small hours. Sometimes their excursions come back empty-handed, at others they are conjurors, pulling out yards and yards of affective scarves from an apparently empty sleeve, showing me (if I will listen) the roots of how I really feel. Even to begin to understand their origin, I need to pursue these images like a hound with my nose to the scent. In this way I come closer to understanding who I am.

While paying attention is easiest if we have an object to focus on, at its heart it does not need an object. Then focusing is separated from attending to: we are looking to cultivate a state of detached awareness, of being. However, to suspend thought and allow oneself to be requires practice, since distractions pop up all the time. The skill lies in learning to recognise these and to refocus gently.

---

111 Claxton G (1997) *Hare Brain and Tortoise Mind: Why intelligence increases when you think less.* London: Fourth Estate.

# Emptying the mind and clearing out projections

One might ask oneself if such a hunt is not just an egocentric hobby. Why bother with the pursuit of a state that at its best can be only partially acquired? From the point of view of becoming a good practitioner, the aim of this domestic spring cleaning is not only to help us to understand ourselves but also to free us from projections, which clutter the view when we come to engage with others. By opening up our personal sensory awareness, we make the practice of 'paying attention to' and 'being present' much easier. While difficult to describe, it can be life-changing. For me, the practice of emptying the mind facilitates awareness of affective change, of the minute flickers in the mind-map supplied by my mirror neurons. Without the brain's cognitive business I become more aware of what is going on in 'not me'.

We listen better if we have an attitude of non-judgmental acceptance and detachment, not detachment from our conversation partners but from our own needs and desires, so that they do not get in the way of real communication. We want to hear what the person's body language is saying.

It is not my intention to put off people who support those on the autistic spectrum by making the process sound too burdensome, but rather to state that for me this way of honing my sensory awareness has added to my ability to put myself alongside my autistic partners (as of course, with any other conversation partner). What we do need is simplicity and openness to the reality that our partners are experiencing, and to value their responses, not seeking to judge their behaviour in the light of our own reality. We have to allow them to be themselves without swamping them with our needs.

There is also a warning: Since there is a narrow gap between attention and fixation, we all need to be able to recognise boundaries, to put our own actions into context, so that we do not overstep the difference between what is 'mine' and what is 'not mine'. This can be a particular difficulty for some people with autism and Asperger's syndrome, such as those with highly developed computer skills, where the ability for dedicated concentration is critical. For example, fascination with the extreme reaches of what is possible has been known to outweigh the unrecognised and disastrous consequences of hacking into Pentagon computer files. One of the challenges we face is to find ways of focusing our autistic companions in the realities of here and now. I suggest that we can best do this by using 'their language' to engage them affectively.

## My partner's world

So far we have talked about our own introspective excursions. Now I need to focus my attention on my partner. Moving from self to other than self is a bit like shifting gear from reverse to forward (and finding that with practice one moves from manual to automatic). It does become much simpler once we have an object to 'attend to', something to explore in sensory terms. But we must also have the desire to do so, the willingness to investigate: 'What makes this tick?' Motivation is sometimes innate, such as when my partner is doing an activity that fascinates me as well. Alternatively, and perhaps more often, it is not so much what they are doing that lures one in but rather a desire to tune in to a partner who is in distress and who could be stabilised by the emotional engagement that using their body language has to offer.

Even if I am not necessarily fascinated by my partner's bead on a string, I am deeply intrigued by their fascination; not just what they are doing but why they are so deeply committed to focusing on this particular activity, and how are they doing it. To answer the first question, doing what they do with them and responding to their movements, I find I am initiated into their qualia, perceiving the colour of the bead, its weight, movement and spin in a way that I had not done previously. However, it would be a mistake to suggest that my motivations are the same as theirs, since the reason for their absorption is defensive. By attending to this object of fascination the person can filter out excess stimuli; they know what they are doing since it is predictable and self-confirming, giving them the certainty they so desperately require: 'It is exactly the same each time'.[112] So the further question I need to ask is: what is it in their environment that is driving them in the direction of total retreat? Why are they so locked in?

Whether we are autistic or not, our brains do not like to be inactive and in the absence of defined objectives will chunter along through daydreams and wishful thinking. Most of us will have experienced perseverance, when our brains will not switch off and the tune in our heads goes round and round without stopping, seemingly unending, but eventually overtaken by something else. However, in people with autism, this perseverance combined with self-defence – keeping the excess baggage of sensory overload at bay – leaves no room for alternatives. This is where people with autism will sit out the sensory siege in which their lives are lived.

It is important to remember that using body language is a two-way process, not something we do to our partners. Not only are we aiming to capture their attention but we have to give full attention ourselves. We are not only reading our partner's initiatives but also using our own body language (sometimes in an exaggerated way) to talk to them.

Gabriel is flicking a piece of string. He is not particularly interested in my mirrored response of what I now suspect is a default activity. Suddenly he notices a minute speck on his trousers – this is where his attention really is. He dives on to it with the ferocity of a hawk onto its prey. Instead of thinking, 'Gabriel is picking at fluff', I am caught up in the intensity of his movement and it is this swooping movement to which I respond. Immediately we are engaged. He gives me all his attention as we share in a mutual activity – his choice, not mine – but the actual behaviour is irrelevant, what matters is our involvement with each other through resonant affect rather than cognition.

Like the waves breaking on the shore, movement, variation and unpredictability clearly raise the level of attention. These are all characteristics of engagements with others. So, in the light of attention, how can we best dispose ourselves to engage with other?

---

112 Barron J & Barron S (1992) *There's a Boy in Here*. New York: Simon and Schuster.

## Chapter 7: A walk by the sea

Consider the sergeant major drilling his recruits:

'Attention!'

Heels clap together, bodies stiffen, hands press into the seams of trousers, eyes facing the front – not the best posture for all round attention, more mono-directional, not asking for thought. He gathers them physically. But it is not until the captain arrives and says, 'At ease, stand easy, gather round', that there is an opportunity for general attention. This is the time to listen. We can compare this compliance with the alert but relaxed attitude of attention within an interactive engagement. Whereas the sergeant major is treating his men like objects, within a dyadic engagement each partner is totally aware not only of themselves but also of the other.

When my autistic partner treats me as an object, brushing me aside like a lump of wood, it is disconcerting. I want to protest: 'This is me in here, trying to reach you out there, each of us engaged in the struggle to make sense of the world around us.' But first we have to notice each other, pick each other out from the sensory ground and claim each other's attention. I can see you but you don't seem to notice me.

However, if I should ask, 'Why won't you to talk to me when I long to talk to you?', I am making two errors. The first assumes that my autistic partner does not want to communicate (with people). The second of my errors is to assume that they experience voices in the same way as I do, that communication is a pleasurable activity. And yet we are told by Jolliffe and others who have autism that this is not true,[113] they do want to communicate but cannot handle the enormous burden this throws onto the processing system.

So as well as paying attention, I need to understand that the ways that I (a neurotypical person) may attempt to engage your attention (as an autistic person), may be interpreted by your brain as threatening, because you do not have the same internal feedback as I do. For example, my smile, which in my language offers welcome and encouragement, may elicit from your internal system physical pain instead of reassurance. I must not predict or judge your

---

113  Jolliffe T, Lansdown R & Robinson C (1992) Autism: a personal account. *Communication* **26** (3) 12–19.

responses based on the experience of my own feedback, since what is pleasurable to me may be uncomfortable to you.

To begin with it may be more difficult than I think to shed my role as carer and what I view as my superior functional capacity ('My brain works better than yours'). While this may or may not be true in a cognitive sense (and in the case of savants such as Stephen Wiltshire it is certainly not true within the boundaries of his genius), such a path leads me away from the excitement of exploring your world as another human, in all its distinction and difference. It will close both of us off from potential and maintain our affective isolation.

# Finding a way in

So in order to find a user-friendly way of entering into a dialogue that will not trigger your distress, I need to attend to what you are doing while at the same time offering initiatives that are sufficiently similar and thus interesting enough to claim your attention. Perhaps more importantly, I need to attend to your responses to my overtures and answer these. As in conversations, I must not rush the process, but must tune in to the rhythm of our exchange, leaving time for consideration. Active (initiating) and passive (listening) roles can be exchanged, you and I taking turns, neither overriding the other.

What I am looking for in your body language is not only what you are doing but also how you are feeling. Some of the clues as to how you are feeling will be obvious – if you are crying for example.

In a discussion on empathy, the psychiatrist and psychotherapist Murray Cox suggests that it involves the emotional knowing of another human being rather than understanding. In 1951, he quotes Rapaport: 'The referents of the terms, "empathy" and "intuition" are ill-defined.'[114]

Writing 40 years later, Cox repeats:

---

114 Rapaport D (1951) *Organisation and Pathology of Thought*. New York: Columbia UNiversity Press.

> *'The concept [of empathy] remains opaque. This may be due to the very nature of the underlying process, which is preverbal and preconscious and thus intangible. A unique phenomena which reason cannot apprehend.'* [115]

How he would have enjoyed the emergent mirror neuron story, which is drawing back the curtain on our human ability to tune into how other people are feeling.

> *'Passion I see is catching, for mine eyes, seeing those beads of sorrow stand in thine, began to water.'* [116]

# Learning to listen to how you feel

There may be some subliminal muscular changes that I do not consciously notice. So in order to pay attention to you to know what you are doing, I must also pay attention to changes in sensation that you engender in me. Coming back to the implications of the mirror neuron work, the paradox is that I need not only to pay outward attention to your movements and listen to your sounds but also to pay intimate attention to what is going on in my own brain. Outwardly, I attend to you with my senses, which allow me to see, feel, and hear what you are doing, but simultaneously I must pay intimate internal attention to my affective map to know how you are feeling. I read your affect, not directly from you but through the mirror map of my own brain. The affective sensation of you that I perceive in my brain is like a page being turned, something different presenting itself.

# Affective language and the mirror map

Although the idea of 'subliminal advertising' is common currency, 'mind reading' has been regarded with suspicion, since until

---

[115] Murray C (2003) In: F Pfäfflin and G Adshead (Eds) *A Matter of Security*. London: Jessica Kingsley Publishers.

[116] Shakespeare W (1599) Julius Caesar 111.1.283. In: Cox M (1995) *Shakespeare as Prompter: The amending imagination in theatre and therapy*. London: Jessica Kingsley Publishers.

recently it has defied rational explanation. However, as Vasu Reddy points out, all of us are being influenced by incoming stimuli below the threshold of sensation or consciousness all the time, images and sounds that affect our mind without us being aware of them. Just because such influences originate in another person, mind reading is not science fiction (me mysteriously looking into your brain) but rather the capacity to take seriously the sensations generated in my brain by my sensory appreciation of your state. When I am working, it may be on reflection some time later that I notice and reflect on the twitch that alerted my brain to a change in the affective state of my partner. But I can improve my ability to read body language by learning to pay attention to any such 'change in feeling' that this 'insidesight' prompts.

So, in attending to my partner I observe what they are doing. In this part of the process I empty my mind of what I feel they ought to be doing and simply listen and watch, immersing myself in the rhythm of the conversation they are having with themselves. I am not only observing their initiatives but also reading the mind-map of affect in my own brain, especially any changes in tone and tension of expression. What does the rhythm of my partner's movements or sounds tell me about how they are feeling? Do I sense any change in their affect? Next I offer actions or sounds based on the physical feedback they are giving themselves, in the hope that these will attract their attention without triggering the stresses that arise from the difficulties of processing. I am trying to shift the person's attention from their inner self-stimulus to conversation, to persuade them to look for the source of 'their sounds', which come from outside of themselves. Backwards and forwards, our shared attention builds into engagement and conversation.

Our exchange is far more than simple imitation or copying and closer to the activity of a jazz musician who takes a theme or mood or maybe just a few notes and extemporises on these. They use these as a baseline and take off. Humphrey Littleton, the famous jazz trumpeter who died recently, talked in terms of being 'alive to the moment', making it up as you go along. In using body language, we engage in a spontaneous duet, adlibbing off each other. To think of this only in terms of copying and imitation limits our freedom.

# The pulling power of discrepancy

The power of small discrepancies in attracting attention is highlighted by recent psychological studies, which show that although 'mirroring' influences subsequent behaviour, mirroring with a slight delay was even more effective. When an experimenter spilled several pens on the floor making it look like an accident, students who had previously been mirrored were two to three times more likely to help pick them up than those who had not.[117] A study by Robin Tanner and Tanys Chartrand, psychologists at Duke University, found that mirroring a person's posture with a one or two second delay was even more effective in influencing a person's subsequent behaviour than synchronous mirroring. They concluded that once the brain has adjusted to the game and can predict what is going to happen (and therefore knows that this does not present a threat) it turns its attention to other potentially more important issues. Their advice is, 'Be a mirror – but a slow and imperfect one'.[118]

# The faulty mirror

It is worth pausing for a minute to consider what we might mean by a bad mirror. Why should an imperfect response be more meaningful in terms of grabbing our attention than a perfect one? If one thinks of a distorting fairground mirror, one immediately understands how attention is lured in by the conjunction of an image that is simultaneously recognisable and alien. We are fascinated by the mismatch and even move our heads around as our brains try to reconcile what we are seeing with what we anticipated. The brain keeps working away trying to resolve the conundrum and meanwhile we are literally transfixed by our inability to marry the illusion with expectation. It is the change, the 'difference', that switches attention into engagement. Is this all right for me? What will happen next?

---

117 Van Baaren RB, Holland RW, Kawakami K & Knippenberg AV (2004). Mimicry and prosocial behavior. *Psychological Science* **15** 71–74.
118 Carey B (2008) You remind me of me. *The New York Times* **12 February.**

# Chapter 8

# Compare and contrast

Many of us will be familiar with the style of examination question that starts, 'Compare and contrast…' and which goes on to present two different situations. The brain drags up one scenario and tries to hold it while ticking boxes in the second. What do they have in common? What are the differences? And do they shed any light on each other at all?

## Brian and Mary

Last week I was asked to work with two completely different people, living in totally different circumstances. I hadn't seen either before. Brian is a man in his 40s with a severe learning disability; Mary is a child of seven. Brian is blind, at least he appears to have no effective sight although he does occasionally open his eyes and roll the whites to the ceiling. He may be able to see shadows but this is only conjecture. Mary is on the autistic spectrum, wrapped in her own world, flitting from one activity to another, frequently extremely distressed. What they have in common is that they are both self-injuring, punching themselves in the face. In both cases this is the reason that I am asked to see if it is possible to help them.

Brian has lived at least 30 years of his life in a long-stay hospital. Those of us who have worked in such institutions will know that even in spite of the efforts of some highly motivated members of staff, this was not normally a happy experience, and it was one that

Chapter 8: Compare and contrast

as a small child, Brian responded to by learning to hit himself. His parents gave him a 'comforter' to try and mitigate his distress, one which he still wraps his hands in. Three years ago he moved out of hospital and is now a tenant in a community home which he shares with three other men. They are supported by a caring team, some of whom have known Brian for a long time. When Brian is distressed, his self-harm can spill over into attacks on those who support him.

The contrast with Mary's background could not be greater. She lives at home with her warm-natured and loving mother Sue. She has a young brother who is 14 months old. Mary's attacks on herself are so violent that she has fractured her fingers in the past and in a separate incident broken her nose. My first contact with Mary and her mother, Sue, was through a letter from Sue describing her appalling struggle to keep Mary from destroying herself and appealing for help.

> *'It breaks my heart watching her hitting herself and not being able to do much about it. I'm often on my knees, crying and pleading with her to stop but she does not understand. She definitely has a pain in her head and she's trying to relieve it by striking herself. She hits her temples and eyebrows constantly.'*[119]

If Sue tries to stop Mary hitting herself with her hands by holding her, Mary leans out and crashes her head against anything solid around her. Sue is literally at the end of her tether, completely exhausted both physically and mentally. She does not know what to do. Neither do Brian's care staff, particularly the women, since he has a habit of grabbing whatever is to hand, which in the case of females may well be the breast.

Apart from their obvious distress, what other links are there between a man with severe visual impairment and a learning disability, and a child at the extreme end of the autistic spectrum who, indications suggest, is possibly more intelligent than she presents?

---

119 Undated personal communication to the author.

# Not knowing

The first and most obvious similarity is that, for different reasons, Brian and Mary do not know what is going on around them and, again for different reasons, are both interpreting their environment as threatening. Brian's eyes are damaged so he is not receiving the information he requires about the world around him; any visual messages from outside fall at the first fence. In addition, his childhood in an institution has almost certainly left him with the need to be on his guard against negative experiences. It is widely thought that about 75% of people with severe learning disabilities in long-stay hospitals were abused in one sense or another. Even if this was not the case, as a blind child, through no fault of his parents, Brian was isolated from everything that offered security. Brian's self-harm indicates that he was anything but happy in an environment he experienced as hostile.

On the other hand, Mary's sight seems to be good. She can spot and pick up what she wants without difficulty. Her eyes work. They pass on the information she receives to her brain. Her problem is her inability to process and put into context all of the incoming messages she receives from the world outside. Taking into account the descriptions offered by people with autism, her brain is stacked up with images, sounds and sensations on the rampage, overlapping and interfering with each other. In order to cope, she fixates on one while the others swirl around like 'glitch on the television'.[120] Donna Williams says, 'If I see the leaf on the tree, I can't see the tree, and vice versa.'[121] Ros Blackburn describes her experience as like looking through a tube, seeing details without their surroundings [122]. And these details are on the move; trying to hold them down is stressful and exhausting. The size of objects can alter without warning. Such distortions are evidence of scotopic sensitivity: a kaleidoscope world, provoked by bright light, certain colours and patterns. Even without specialist colorimetric tests, some of the indications of such a condition are that an individual screws up their eyes in bright light and shows a preference for or a dislike of certain colours. (The preference is an indication that processing is easier in certain colour lights – in Mary's case, green

---
120  *A is for Autism* (1992) Film. Directed by Tim Webb. London: Fine Take Productions with Channel 4.
121  Williams D (1995) *Jam Jar*. Film. Fresh Film in association with Channel 4, UK.
122  Blackburn R (2002) Flint NAS seminar. 16 July 2002.

is her preferred colour.) The child lives under the shadow of being overwhelmed, with the terrifying consequences of the autonomic storm (an event that can happen many times a day). For some people simply changing the colour of the light bulb can modify distress but since the symptoms do not show up in an ordinary eye test specialist help and colorimetric tests are essential.

## Using touch for orientation

Since they are both having problems with knowing what is happening, both Brian and Mary use touch to orientate themselves, but there are subtle differences. When he is moving around in his bedroom Brian feels his bed, running his hands over the quilt and feeling along the side. On the other hand, one of Mary's behaviours is to patrol the room, touching the walls or running her hands up and down the banisters in very specific places. In her case she does know where she is but she is trying to make sense of the rest of the world. Is it in the place where she knows it ought to be or has it moved? Both Brian and Mary know what they are looking for but Brian wants to know where he is in relation to the world outside. However, since her experience is that it is on the move, Mary wants to know where the world is in relation to her.

## Marking out territory

At this point I want to reach back into my own childhood and explore the feelings associated with a related issue to see if they throw any light on Mary's behaviour. I was brought up during the war in a military service family and we moved house frequently. Sometimes we only stayed in one place for a matter of weeks before uprooting and moving on again. We did have a house of our own by the edge of a marshy creek, but this was in a Coastal Regulation Zone, so it was rarely that we were able to get there – and then it was only for short periods.

These fleeting visits were precious islands of pleasure in an unpredictable procession of removal vans. When we tumbled out of the car, I would rush round the house. This was home; this was where I belonged, where 'I' was. Leaving a few days later was accepted as inevitable but I developed what, even then, seemed to me the curious habit of walking around my room and kissing each wall before I left, refusing to leave before I had finished my circuit and having to start again if interrupted.

Why on earth should I do this? What was I after? Having distanced myself from such a routine it seems absurd and the feeling of contentment is elusive. This attempt to pull it out of its drawer feels embarrassing but here it is: need and shame, raw affect, pain. It is much easier to keep it locked up. However, staying with the papered wall, the texture is slightly rough, I can feel it in my fingers now and I can see the dull cream paint. Now I am a surveyor, triangulating the different senses. Vision, touch – through those most sensitive tactile organs, the lips – and even smell substantiate the wall. I performed this ritual, in the spurious certainty that when I returned it would still be there.

In retrospect, against a background of nomadic turmoil, this was a child searching for permanence, not just of a building but of self. It made her feel secure. Fortunately for her, she grew beyond the need for this ceremony; the security became built-in, internalised, but at the time it was a lifeline.

If we return now to Mary and her autism, we find a child whose cognitive awareness is a complete shambles. Nothing is permanent, everything is elusive and keeps slipping away. Marking out her territory in this shape-shifting confusion is one way of searching for stability, but the disorder remains. Unable to switch off, her brain perseverates, continuing to feed her with distorted messages and hence, anxiety. When she performs her routines she knows what she is doing. Jolliffe tells us that she spends her whole life trying to make sense of what is happening.[123] What we see as compulsive behaviour has become part of Mary's heroic struggle against chaos, an attempt to still the kaleidoscope so that she can make out the underlying pattern.

---

123 Jolliffe T, Lansdown R & Robinson C (1992) Autism: a personal account. *Communication* **26** (3) 12–19.

Chapter 8: Compare and contrast

# Reducing stress

To generalise, the manner in which people with autism perform these routines gives us a clue as to their levels of anxiety. The more stressed they are, the more determined their efforts to complete the circuit or whatever task they have set themselves. For example, a man with severe autism and behavioural disorder patrols the walls of a noisy day centre all day, touching the walls in certain places. If this repetitive behaviour is in any way interrupted he goes berserk, roaring with fury and striking out at anybody within range. His behaviour is that of someone who is fighting for his life. In a sense that is what is happening. His body's self-defence system has been triggered. As far as he is concerned his protective shield is down and he is in life-threatening danger. Everything he has is mobilised for self-protection.

From the point of view of the person on the autistic spectrum, one of the most important functions of these behaviours is self-preservation against sensory havoc. If we interrupt the person we remove this safeguard and leave them exposed to what they experience as the possibility of extinction. Donna Williams says that it felt like death coming to get her.[124] Both she and Gunilla Gerland describe the appalling rise of neural sensations starting with a fizzy feeling in the back of the head and spreading into the limbs, 'like cracks in an earthquake and death coming to get me.' [125]

Building defences against anxiety does not deal with it, it is still rattling around in the psyche. So our question now becomes, can we find a way of reducing affective stress as well as that caused by the overloading senses of vision, sound and touch? Will reducing the anxiety, relieve the need for such obsessional rites?

Rather than hoping to breach the defensive wall that our partners have retreated behind, we have to find another way of getting through to them, one that does not set off the alarm bells. The problem is that almost everything we offer simply adds to their confusion. So, what camouflage can we adopt that will enable us to

---

124 Williams D (1998) *Somebody Somewhere: Breaking free from the world of autism*. London: Jessica Kingsley Publishers.
125 Williams D (1998) *Somebody Somewhere: Breaking free from the world of autism*. London: Jessica Kingsley Publishers.

'talk' to Brian and Mary in ways that have meaning for them and which allow us to tune into each other, we into their world and they into ours?

Looking first at the physical problems, Brian is really cut off from what is going on around him. Not only is this lonely but also, if much of what he has experienced of interaction with his environment in the past has been threatening, his reactions are likely to be defensive in the form of aggression.

# Aggression

No matter how good our intentions, it is sometimes difficult to maintain our calm in the face of what seems to be a personal attack. Such attacks present us with two different questions. The first is: what do I do about this now when Johnny is rushing me? The second relates to why Johnny feels the need to do such a thing? The trouble is that on the whole, solutions to 'difficult to manage' behaviour have tended to focus on how we cope with and control people, rather than the underlying triggers.

# Addressing the roots of distressed behaviour

Traditionally, management strategies have gone down one of two avenues. The first ignores 'maladaptive behaviours'. The second (behavioural alternative), treats the behaviour as one that can be corrected by using 'reward' and 'restraint' – and what is still sometimes thought of as 'punishment' – the carrot and stick approach. Punishment ranges from the relatively benign withdrawal of privileges to, in the past, physical interventions of an abusive nature. Unfortunately, even if they do succeed, neither of these strategies actually addresses the root causes of the behaviour. Even the term now in common usage, 'challenging behaviour', sets us up in opposition to our partner.

# Fear

In my experience of engaging with people with severe learning disabilities and at the extreme end of the autistic spectrum, I have found that very few are 'naughty'; they do not have the necessary manipulative skills. In the case of adults with severe learning disabilities, we are sometimes still trying to engage with people who have been incarcerated in long-term hospitals, a number of whom have been abused or traumatised in one way or another. In many cases the environment itself was abusive, noisy, unloving and restrictive. Our partners learned survival skills to protect themselves and much of their current behaviour speaks to us of long-term damage in the past. This is about pathways of fear: 'If I thump you, you will keep away from me.' I have learned to do this as a precaution even if you have no hostile intent, just as a warning.

The trouble with the more benign of these approaches – ignoring a difficult behaviour – is that it does not always work; although in the absence of alternatives such programmes are often continued in the face of failure. For example, a man shouts humiliating abuse at his support partner every day. It is public and it hurts, but the policy is that his carer should ignore it. When the carer asks me what they should do about this, I question how long this has been going on. They reply, 'six months'. When I suggest to them that such a length of time suggests that the strategy is not effective, they are surprised. The point of this story is that it is often easier to carry on with an unsuccessful approach than to sit down and think outside of the box. Inertia is simpler than change. Is there any other way we should be addressing this problem?

# Interpreting behaviour in the light of our own reality

Brian has moods. There are times when he is more irritable than others, biting his hand, slapping himself and kicking himself. He can communicate in the sense that he lets people know what he wants, or more often what he does not want. For example, once he is up and walking (which has to be assisted), it is hard to get him to sit down; he simply refuses to do so. His gait is very unstable and he lurches around on the arm of his support partner. Like many people who are blind, he grabs anything to hold on to it. When he grabs women's breasts they are soft, like a cushion. They do not offer much in the way of support, so he grabs harder and now has found that, in a world that is not giving him meaningful responses, this is a way of getting them.

It is easy to interpret this behaviour as sexually motivated but the time I witness this behaviour Brian seems confused, since not everyone offers him the consistent support he needs when walking. Some staff walk beside him and he is able to place both hands on their arm. The problem with this strategy is that, although it seems more normal, Brian is so unsteady that he leans extremely heavily on the person who is guiding him – a position it is difficult to maintain. Others walk backwards in front of him, holding one hand in each of theirs so that he achieves a better balance. The time I saw him grab was when the previous support partner had used the one arm method, which involved putting both of his hands on her arm. However, the next support partner was trying to take both his hands separately. Expecting one support position Brian put out both hands to take her arm but what he encountered was her face-on. When his hands met her breasts it seemed the result of confusion rather than of potential assault.

The reason that I have described this in detail is that we very often interpret behaviour according to our own experience of reality rather than that of our partner. While the reason in this case may be either sexual or Brian's instability, perhaps we should at least check whether or not offering him a consistent support position reduces the incidence of such an unwanted activity. In a blind world that does not answer him in a way that has meaning (and since this behaviour does at least get him some sort of response), will finding an alternative and significant way of engaging Brian also help reduce his need to pinch?

# Using Brian's language

When I meet Brian he is sitting in an easy chair. He is sitting on his hands, which are wrapped in their comforter, and he has slipped down so that his backside rests on the edge of the seat with his legs in the air. This is his preferred position and all it offers in the way of potential connection are his feet. So I try rubbing his toes when he makes a sound. He swings his legs away. His support partner on the opposite side of the chair does the same. He swings them back again. Maybe he is trying to avoid our attention, but no, when I deliberately miss out on my turn, he swings them back to her for more. Backwards and forwards, grinning and eventually, laughing. How long is it since Brian had fun? Here is something he can interact with and to some extent, control. Later on, I try working with his sounds, firstly using a kazoo to answer them and finally settling down to a long 'conversation' (about half an hour) during which he tries out a number of different sounds using his tongue.

# Brian's joke

When Brian is distressed, his sounds increase to a bellow. The policy is that these should be ignored. However, when I am using his sounds to communicate with him he starts to increase them and it is clear to those of us present that he is deliberately testing how far he can go. (One of Brian's most attractive characteristics is his sense of humour.) He tries out louder sounds which relate to those he makes when he is disturbed. I continue to answer these with lower sounds and different rhythms and eventually he breaks out into laughter. It is quite clear to me and to his staff that Brian is testing us, pushing his luck to see if I will 'chicken out' and he is delighted that I continue to respond in a way that has meaning for him. An intervention that could have gone either way ends in a shared joke. His house staff team say that he is calmer than normal for the rest of the day. He has not hit himself once while I have been with him. The point that I am trying to make is that if we stick to trying to control our partner's behaviour, or alternatively ignoring it, we do not address their underlying distress. Even if we manage to check it temporarily, such behaviour is likely to continue. If we are going to change this pattern, what we need to address is not so much the conduct but the feelings that underpin it. The first steps are to try and unravel why our partner is upset. What are they trying to gain through their unhappy behaviour?

## Using vibration with Mary

Like Brian, Mary has also learned to be afraid, not of what actually happens to her but of what her brain tells her is happening – the pseudo-messages that speak of total confusion and the sensory overload that constantly threatens to overwhelm her. In order to cut down on sensory input Mary often sits or walks around under a quilt. She tries to bring order into her world by hitting herself – at least when she does this she knows what she is doing. Lindsey Weekes tells us that he was so afraid of going into the autonomic storm he would do anything to try to prevent it: run in front of a car or beat his head against the wall.[126] Often Mary's face is badly bruised; when we met, she had a fading black eye.

Mary's mum, Sue, is an exceptionally warm and caring mother and has been trying very hard to interact meaningfully with Mary. As she herself acknowledges, this has not been supported by any real understanding of the nature of Mary's autism. For example, however lovingly intended, speech (for example, trying to soothe her when she is becoming upset) can add to the processing problems that are experienced by a child who is becoming distressed. And restraint (for example, holding her arms when she is hitting her face) can increase stress levels because this is the way that the child has developed to best cope with the confusion and pain she is experiencing.

Having noted that Mary orientates herself through touching the walls, and thus that pressure has meaning for her, I introduce vibration to see if this will bring her out from under her blanket to interact. (Not having vibration equipment with me I use electric toothbrushes – two, so that we maintain the possibility of interaction.[127]) Her response is immediate, she is fascinated by them. We hand them to each other. Now her face is alert and lively as she puts her hand out to take one from me. She is laughing and cuddling up to me and eventually gives me a kiss. She soon learns to turn them on and off. However, although we are sharing the

---

[126] Weekes L (date unknown) *A Bridge of Voices*. Documentary radio programme. London: BBC Radio 4. Produced by Tim Morton for Sandpoint Programs.

[127] Electric toothbrushes, which are a cheap and handy source of vibration, come in two varieties with fixed or removable heads. Choose one with a fixed head since those with removable heads have a sharp metal spike if the head is pulled off.

game, at this stage the principal focus of her attention is on the toothbrushes as objects rather than interpersonal attention to me as subject.

Watching her carefully under the edge of her quilt, I see that when Mary's hands are free she spends her time pressing her thumb on the tip of her index finger. She also bends and flexes her fingers and watches her hand movements. Now that she is happy for me to sit beside her on the sofa, I gently insert my thumb into her fingers and press on her fingertips. Although she does not look at me she starts to pay attention deeply, focusing on what we are doing together. This is interesting since recent research has shown that it is not so much the direction of gaze that is important, but rather, where attention is focused: 'the attentional spotlight' is separate from and can be ahead of the direction of gaze.[128]

We are probably familiar with situations where a person we are talking to seems distant while we are explaining something. Charged with this, they may respond, 'I was just thinking about it,' or, 'I was just trying to sort something out.' A feature of such incidents is that the person seems to have withdrawn into themselves, their attention is internally directed on what they are thinking or feeling. We, the watchers will also have been drawn into this inner point of focus. As a colleague who was observing the interaction between me and Mary said: 'The room became totally quiet. You could hear a pin drop.'

A picture of Mary taken at this point captures her peeping out from under her quilt. While she is not looking at me, the expression on her face is both attentive and apprehensive. She has noticed my intervention in her hand-game conversation with herself; her interest has been aroused but she has not yet made up her mind whether she should interpret this intrusion as friendly or not. She is feeling her way into a new situation: 'This is my signal but I didn't make it.'

Mary's brain has been alerted by change. This is a pause period of assessment. A 'hang on a minute while I think about this' moment.

[128] Kuhn G, Tatler B, Findlay J & Cole G (2008) Misdirection in magic: implications for the relationship between eye gaze and attention. *Visual Cognition* **16** (2) 391–405.

Her brain is Googling for fresh information, anything that will give her bearings on her familiar but apparently displaced signals. She hovers on the brink before deciding what to do.

# The moment of decision

In order to survive we are constantly on watch, sifting the sensory evidence as it comes in and assessing it against our own experiences: 'Is this good for me or bad for me?' At any given instant we are dealing with countless incoming sensory stimuli, making decisions and reacting, deciding which need our attention. In a biological sense we are totally self-centred, looking for any changes in the sensory stream, anything that warrants further investigation and anything that has potential for advantage or threat.

If the incoming message is urgent enough, our reaction may be an instinctive, 'I never-gave-it-a-thought' knee-jerk response, intended to remove us from the perceived life-threatening dangers of an impending situation. But sometimes the potential outcome of a situation is not presented in black and white and needs conscious assessment. 'Do we or do we not pay attention to this and what, if any, are the threats or possible advantages to be avoided or gained by engaging with this?'

We call this 'the moment of decision', but really it is the 'moment before decision', when everything irrelevant is shut out so that we can concentrate all our resources on the particular input that is puzzling us. Perceived by the onlooker as stillness, in an effort to decode the potential meaning of the stimulus, we are searching deeper and deeper for its source, the 'ah, there it is' recognition and its concomitant release of tension.

# The attentional spotlight

In such a sensory conversation the attentional spotlight seems to be inwardly directed. At this point of stillness it appears that our partner is 'listening' to their own affective stream, immersed in what they are feeling. Such is the power of concentration that we are totally riveted too. In this case we feel the depths of Mary's attention and we are all moved.

The scenario changes: in the next photograph, Mary is holding back the edge of her quilt and focusing on my hands, touching and exploring them with hers. Her face, while still attentive, has lost its apprehension and this is replaced by a relaxed interest in what we are doing together.

# Validating negative feelings, accepting distress

Returning to misbehaviour, what is very clear and perhaps unusual for a child with autism is that Mary is demonstrably fond of her mother. She spends a lot of time cuddled up to her and during my intervention she constantly refers back to her. For example, after playing the hand game with me she returns to Sue and holds out her hand, obviously she now wants to try it out with her mother. However, it is clear from the level of her demand that besides wanting to interact in a way that demonstrates affection, there is also a great deal of 'need'. This resembles the demand for attention of a much younger child and I suggest that, while Sue has given Mary a lot of speech-based attention, what has been missing are signals that are easily accessible to Mary, ones that her brain can take on board and manage without elaborate processing.

It is towards the end of our visit and Mary is starting to get restless. Watching a replay of the film it is clear that this happens at a time when we have stopped interacting with Mary and are talking over her to her mother. Her reaction to this is very interesting. At first she walks over and stands by Sue and tries to continue playing the finger-hand game with her. When Sue does not respond (because she is talking to us), Mary moves quickly across the room and knocks one of the audio speakers over. We pick it up, but still Sue does not return to the hand game Mary wants to play. It is absolutely clear that having lost our interest, Mary is desperate for her mother's attention. So she takes additional action, flipping over a low coffee table and immediately looking at her mother, seeing if this will provoke a reaction. Mary is not purposely misbehaving, but rather seeking any means possible to regain the safety net of her mother's earlier responsiveness. The underlying problem is that in spite of Sue's best efforts to communicate, Mary is lacking in significant contact.

Sue tells us that in the past, before she began to understand the distress caused by Mary's autism, at this stage in the escalation of 'misbehaviour' she would have tapped Mary's hand and told her she was naughty, a punishment practice she discontinued some time ago. However, the pattern seems to be firmly embedded in Mary's brain. She walks over to her mother and in an ingrained gesture, holds out her hand and says, 'Naughty girl'. But the way Mary says these words sounds detached, as if she knows they relate to the situation but does not understand what 'naughty' is. While linked to the situation, she is disassociated from its affective component. What is predominant in her mind is that she has lost contact with her mother who is the rock and point of stability in her turbulent life, and this is causing her deep distress. I suggest that when this happens again, instead of punishment, Sue should think in terms of addressing this distress, validating how Mary feels, and that the best way to do this would be to take her by the hand, give it a kiss and 'rub it better'.

Contrary to what one might suppose, validating negative feelings addresses the hurt and frequently the undesirable behaviour drops away. It tells the person they are loved for themselves and not just conditionally if they are good. In people with autism who are verbal or semi-verbal, the palpable relaxation that comes with such an acknowledgement is evident in calm, relieved voices as their tension drains.

Once Sue starts to use responses that relate to the repetitive behaviours in Mary's body language, her distress is reduced and she begins to respond in quite a different way: she is relaxed and looking round to see what is happening. For example, her mother reports that during supper in the evening, Mary started to huff and display anxiety. She hit herself once, hard, but Sue kept cool and answered her sounds and movements, guided her up the stairs, still responding using her sounds. Mary calmed, sat on her bed exploring a book she had not looked at in more than a year, smiled, pulled the covers over her, went to sleep and slept soundly for eight hours.

Throughout our visit, Sue saw Mary's behaviour as unusually calm. At no point did she attempt to hit herself, which normally happens daily. As the day progressed, her eye contact and her desire for proximity increased. She was very relaxed, looking around at her surroundings in an interested way. When we returned after lunch she looked up and clearly recognised both myself and my colleague, looking from one to the other.

# Relaxation and improving speech

One of the outcomes of Intensive Interaction is to reduce anxiety by providing our partner's brain with stimuli that do not require elaborate processing. This allows abilities that may have previously been seen as 'weak' or 'nonexistent' to emerge. This is certainly the case here with regards to Mary's language. The shift in her verbal ability has exceeded even my expectation in that her speech improved dramatically from muttered, near unintelligible and learnt phrases in the morning, to intelligible, relevant speech which had not been evident before. This shift was observed during our visit and was reported by her mother to continue during the two days after our departure.

In a conversation during a lunchtime break, we had considered that Mary's ability to talk might be only minimal and perhaps ineffective as a means of spontaneous communication. However, while we were away, Mary's grandmother phoned her mother Sue and over the phone heard Mary quite clearly ask for 'cream cheese', something she had never said before. (Normally her grandmother is unable to understand anything Mary says.) On the second evening Sue commented to Mary as she put her to bed that the children in the street were making a noise. Mary replied unexpectedly, 'What a noise', using different words and intonation from her mother. She had not simply copied her mother, but had supplied a novel and relevant reply. A few minutes later, as Sue departed from the bedroom, Mary said, 'I love you'. In doing so she not only expressed her feeling but also, clearly demonstrated her connectedness with how she feels – something that is commonly supposed to be impossible for children on the autistic spectrum.

# Chapter 9

# 'Happiest days of your life'

*(Nothing in this chapter is in any way intended to be critical of the many schools that welcome me, but simply to point to some of the practical difficulties that both teachers and children have to cope with.)*

## The National Curriculum

A teacher addresses her class: 'Today we are going to do maths.' The children in their wheelchairs, who have multiple physical disabilities and/or complex needs, do not stir. There is not a movement in their bodies or a flicker on their faces. The words are sounds that drift over their heads without significance. The only interest shown at all is by a child with autism who grabs the felt cut-out number when it is brought round and flaps it wildly. Simply put, there is no connection at all between what it is that has meaning for us and what the children's brains can take on board. Afterwards, I ask the teacher how much of what she is presenting she thinks is taken in by her pupils. She answers sadly, 'Nothing, but what am I to do? I have to teach the National Curriculum.'

# Teaching: a sensory model for children with autism

What are we doing in the name of education? This is a good school. Its teachers are loving and caring. What is amiss in this and the classes for so many children with extreme disabilities in special schools, is not the dedication of the staff – and even their ingenuity in trying to carry out an irreconcilable task – but an education system that totally disregards the perceptual problems experienced by children with very severe sensory disabilities, either of the body or, since they are less visible, those of a faulty processing system in the brain. In our desperation to bring them into our world we are totally ignoring what it is that these children's brains can recognise.

For example, even if a child's deafness is diagnosed (a situation that cannot be taken for granted), it is so easy to for us to gloss over the implications of their perceptual limitations, since it involves a radical shift from our own sensory experience and how we have learned to relate to the world about us. To understand that other people's experience of reality may truly be different to our own involves letting go of all the rules we have devised to orientate ourselves vis-à-vis what is other than ourselves. This leap in imagination is one of the hardest things to teach.

So for those of us who do not consider ourselves disabled, let us bring this idea within our realm of experience. A child with short-sightedness (myopia) says to her mother, who has been reproaching her for her lack of attention, 'Mum, I really can't see what you see.' Her mother, a teacher, tells me that this is the first time that she has been able to take on board the difference between her visual experience and that of her daughter. What is clear to her in her world is, if visible at all, fuzzy and indistinct for her daughter. We understand that a child with myopia has a physical problem seeing things but she is not in any sense labelled as having a learning disability. What is the actual difference between her and a child with autism, one of whose major problems may be that of hypersensitivity to light and processing visual images, known as 'Irlen syndrome' or 'scotopic sensitivity'? How does this differ from a condition that the majority of us all will experience sooner or later as we fumble for the glasses we have put down somewhere and cannot find without them?

Take a child with autism, whose eyes are screwed up in bright light and who avoids direct eye contact. The physical argument runs as follows.[129]

A child with autism experiences sensory overload: a distressing state, involving erratic feedback from the autonomic nervous system with all its painful and confusing sensations. In order to cut down on sensory intake, if possible the child avoids bright light by closing their eyes and avoiding direct eye contact. To us it appears that they are not interested in us or what we have to offer but there is a physical and fascinating reason for this response.

All of us, autistic or not, receive visual intake on a layer of light-sensitive cells at the back of the eyeball known as the retina. These convert the image received in the form of light waves into electrical impulses that are passed to the brain. These cells are of two types: cones and rods. Cones respond to bright light and colour perception (except red). Rods are activated by (mainly), monochrome vision in poor light. About half of the cones are situated in a relatively tiny depression known as the foveal pit. This is the centre of acute vision and is used when we look directly at objects. Pete Coia suggests that in terms of relative size, one should think of the fovea as the hole in the centre of a golf course green, with the rest of the retina represented by the green plus the fairway. As one fans out from the foveal pit to the edges of the retina, there are more rods but the cones become less dense, since the 50% that are not sunk in the fovea are scattered over a wide area. So, avoiding direct vision immediately cuts down on 50% of visual intake. And if cutting down on visual intake reduces the sensory distortions and pain experienced as a result of hyperactive responses of the autonomic nervous system by half, then avoiding direct eye contact with the world outside and using peripheral vision is the best way of doing this.

So, just as in people with short-sightedness, what happens here in some people with autism is a physical problem, resulting in an avoidance reaction to cut down on sensory distress. While it requires a colorimetric test, it is a condition that can, like short-

---

129 I am wholly indebted to Pete Coia, friend, colleague and handy encyclopaedia, for the details of the following explanation as to what is happening in visual terms for the child (or adult) in this predicament.

sightedness, be relieved by the introduction of coloured lenses (or lighting if the person is not able to wear glasses).

The same goes for the auditory booms and fade-outs that people on the spectrum may experience. Hypersensitivity to sound (hyperacusis) can be acutely painful but can be relieved by reduction of the specific frequencies that trigger such distortions.

What is needed is a sensory model of autism, one that sees the condition in terms of the effects it has on the sensory experience of the child and not in judgmental terms of their secondary behaviour as it affects us. This requires a radical shift in our perception of autism, from seeing a child as 'naughty' or 'attention seeking', (both terms that have been offered to me during this week of writing), to one that understands that they are trying to make sense of the world around them. We have to understand that their apparent rejection of us is part of their desperate struggle to understand what is going on in their environment. Our job is to reduce the 'chatter' from sensory overload, which can cause distress and pain.

Once this autistic overload has been reduced, we can begin to see if there really is a learning disability. A 15-year-old boy squints when he looks into bright light. A colorimetric test shows that he has Irlen syndrome and that his brain processes input more easily when he is wearing blue lenses. He emails me: 'I cannot believe how much difference my glasses have made to my sight. I used to be in the slow lane at school but now I am in the talented stream and my teachers cannot keep up with me.' [130]

So often we speak of a child not paying attention in class and it is true: they sit in their chair looking vacantly into space, totally unconnected with the world round them. 'Poor thing. It's their learning disability.' But when we place our mouths close to their ear, or use a kazoo to enrich sounds, or whisper to cut the sounds down, or try communicating in a high or low voice, their face lights up and they turn towards us with a big grin. Another child, sitting in fluorescent lighting with their eyes screwed up, repetitively flaps a piece of paper. If it is taken away they become desperately

---

[130] Irlen syndrome affects the brain's ability to process visual information. It does not show up in an ordinary eye test and requires a colorimetric test. The colour of the lenses needed is specific to the individual.

agitated, screaming and hitting themselves. Yes, it is known that they are autistic, but we do not take into account the confusion and pain triggered by hypersensitivity to light. In the name of disability we write off the underlying sensory experience and attempt to push all children through a 'one-size-fits-all' system, one with which the child fails to connect.

Part of the reason for this may be that the very severely disabled are, or historically have been, almost invisible. Bussed to and from home and respite centre, they often lack a public life, partly because of behavioural reactions and partly because of physical frailty. Admittedly their reception in the non-disabled world is now more tolerant than it used to be; nevertheless, one suspects that those who draw up curricula are not always familiar with the implications of trying to gain attention from children whose experience of life is of an inner world of silence or confusion. Children who, if they are low on proprioceptive messages, may have little idea where their bodies are, or who, in the case of those with hypersensitivity, are very often in real physical pain. What can we do about this? Is there a way of bringing the light to these children's eyes, to motivate and engage with them?

In some ways the problem is simple. A child who is desperate to get into a dark room and fights off their teacher when they try to prevent them, is simply telling us that they are hypersensitive to light – a painful condition. A child with their hands over their ears is saying that sound hurts (or sometimes that at least if they do this they cut down on some of the sensory input). Either way, pain, or simply 'I want out', we must learn to read and analyse our partner's body language (and this includes behaviour) in the light of the sensory reality they experience and not that of our own. (We would not deliberately hurt a child and yet, through ignorance, our actions are sometimes triggering real pain.)

# A multicultural setting

We are in a multicultural school in an urban setting. This is my first visit and I have never met the children before. I am accompanied throughout the day by the school psychologist, who films our interventions. I am told that there are 27 languages spoken and that this is just in the staff room. Quite a large proportion of the children are autistic, many severely so. Teachers say they are unable to reach some of them. And no matter how caring and diligent the staff members are, it is difficult to claim the attention of, let alone teach, a child who sits in the corner of the room rocking and crying, chasing shadows, tapping bottles on the floor or endlessly feeling their fingers. Interruptions to these activities distress them. They have opted out of a world that seems threatening and incomprehensible.

# Cultural differences in body language

The advantages of using body language are immediately obvious in this situation. We will be using a communication pathway that is common to all of us. Although we do to some extent need to distinguish between features of our partner's body language that are innate (developing as part of a self-stimulatory system in response to the need to seek and maintain coherence) and those laid on top (embedded as part of a specific culture, varying according to ethnic origin). In the latter case we cannot always assume that gestures that we are familiar with mean the same as they do to those we are speaking to. For example, an English teacher tells me of the confusion she has caused by demanding that a student from Ghana looks at her when she speaks – an action which the child would have been taught is rude. A businessman from Japan wonders how he can trust an Englishman who apparently does not know how to keep his face still. A Sikh social worker explains that while his explosive consonants may sound rude to us, he expresses feeling through delicate hand movements. It is very easy to project the habits of our own culture onto our partners.

Nevertheless, while there may be cultural variations it is not so much what our partners do, as how they do it (the bodily posture and facial expression that accompany their sounds or movements) that helps us to tune into their world. The type of fixated behaviours in which the children have taken refuge, the flapping hands, tapping bricks, dribbling, patting sand and so on, are not likely to be those that will have been subject to cultural pressure.

# A difficult place in sensory terms

For a child who needs auditory and visual tranquility, school is a difficult place, primarily because of the number of people with all the different stimuli they present. Every time we move we change shape and each different shape needs reprocessing. We make sounds and demands that children with autism do not understand. In this busy environment bells ring, rooms echo, walls are covered with bright stimulating paintings and worksheets. Strip lighting hurts the eyes and bounces off of shiny surfaces. Voices are booming or slip away. Break-time is a ready-made nightmare ('I thought I was going to go mad' [131]).

# Rico, proprioception and hypersensitivity to sound

We start the day with Rico, who is severely autistic. At the best of times, Rico finds it difficult to sit with his classmates and in this particular room the false ceiling is low and it is very noisy. Due to staff sickness two classes have to be taught in the same room. Temporary difficulties, but how do you explain this to a child who is hypersensitive to sound and whose classmates are also reacting to the overcrowding by shouting and running around expressing their discomfort? Rico withdraws to a corner, hugs a cushion and rocks, making small crying sounds. The more distressed he is the louder his sounds become. Even when he is in his own classroom he will not come and sit with the other children in circle time.

When I make a sound close to Rico's right ear, he flinches in a way that suggests it is painful, an indication that at least one of the sensory stimuli that Rico is hypersensitive to is sound. When I sit near him hugging a cushion Rico turns to me briefly when I tap the wall to the rhythm of his rocking and make his sounds but

---

131 *A is for Autism* (1992) Film. Directed by Tim Webb. London: Fine Take Productions with Channel 4.

eventually we decide that the room really is too noisy (for myself as much as Rico, since even I can no longer distinguish his sounds from the general level of background hubbub). He does not want to come with us when we try to move him but he half rises, so I pick up his chair and take it to the door. Now that he can see what we intend to do he follows us and we lead him to a quieter room next door where he becomes much more interactive. I vary the pitch of my sounds to answer his and he slows down and looks at me. When I play with the cushion in a variety of ways, he smiles. When I copy him, scratching the texture of the cushion, he laughs and then copies my movement. After a while he gets up and walks over to hanging curtains at the entrance to a quiet area. He places one over each shoulder and grasping them with his hands, leans forward on them and pulls himself to and fro, rocking sharply. He also turns himself on a rotating office chair. These jerks and swings suggest that Rico is using activities to activate his vestibular system in a way that is meaningful for him. When Rico bounces, in the face of auditory distress and overload he has a strong overriding signal that tells him what he is doing. This is confirmed when in reply to my enquiries I am told that he enjoys swings and sessions on the trampoline.

Apart from the pleasure that Rico derives from me using his body language with him, reading it as we go along and responding to him in a way that his brain is able to interpret, enables me to decode some of the environmental factors that are disturbing him. In seeing him come out of his inner refuge we share his pleasure even if briefly.

In the longer term, I suggest that on arrival at school in the morning, instead of bringing Rico straight from his transport into a noisy hall, staff should guide him in through a quiet side door. Before being taken to his classroom, Rico should be given 10 minutes on the trampoline to try and help his vestibular problems (rather than using it as an occasional activity to which he clearly relates). The outcome of this is that Rico no longer suffers the painful sensory overload and visual confusion, and after a burst of strenuous physical activity he is able to sit with the circle-time group. This may seem a small step towards integration but it is the outward sign of an enormous change in perception and trust: instead of experiencing chaos, Rico now knows what he is doing.

# Lara

So many children (and adults) with severe autism, whose visual and auditory world is falling apart, take refuge in touch and pressure to maintain at least some consistent link with the world around them. They touch walls, press and scratch their fingers and surfaces, or manipulate their hands: 'When I do this I know what I am doing.' One such child is Lara, whose behaviour is volatile. She is liable to hit out, so it is important to find ways of engaging her attention to promote friendly behaviour. When I first see her she is sitting in a TEACCH work station. Her teacher has two stacks of related flashcards that need to be matched. Lara has been taught this activity for just over a week. She is sitting quietly and her teacher says that she can match a pair if she finds the subject interesting, for example, an orange and a glass of juice. However her teacher's voice does change when she comes to the 'right' match, so Lara is receiving an auditory body language clue as well as a visual clue. Revisiting the film, while Lara is doing the task her face looks bored, switched off. Although she is complying with the requirement to sit still and 'work', she is not involved. As soon as her teacher lifts her attention for a second, Lara picks up one of the stiff plastic cards at random and flexes it in her hand. She is clearly fascinated by the physical sensation she derives from this.

Picking up on this clue, I notice that when Lara is not required to attend she drifts off into a world of self-stimulation that involves scratching one hand with the other. I sit beside her and gradually join in her activity with my own fingers. We take turns and refer back to each other in a conversation that clearly engages her attention, switching it from the inner world that she normally inhabits to interest in the source of a stimulus that her brain can easily process. She becomes emotionally engaged, alert, smiling, laughing and interested in our interaction, so much so that a colleague viewing the film thinks she is a different child from the one previously seen sitting at her desk. Her attention is so marked that she is almost unrecognisable.

The question we have to ask is not just how teachers can maintain this lively interest and use it to enhance their teaching but also how they can use it to make Lara's world more intelligible for her so that she is not anxious and feeling the need to attack those near her. We need to find ways of working 'through' what we call compulsive behaviours rather than working in opposition to them.

## Abu, Ryan, Jaleel and Ahmad: finding coherence through tapping

Four other children are also apparently deriving coherence from tapping. However, here we are going to have to look more closely at exactly what stimulus each child is getting out of their activities, since it is unexpectedly different for each. The question we have to ask ourselves is, exactly what is the sensory feedback that each individual child is using to talk to themselves?

Abu, who has autism and Down's syndrome, is drumming an empty plastic bottle on the floor. The fact that he is deaf means that it is probable that much of the pleasurable sensory feedback he is giving himself derives from the rhythmic jerk he feels in his wrist rather than the noise. Admittedly, he does take note when my colleague bangs loudly on the floor with her bottle, but sound is probably secondary to proprioceptive impact. Following this lead, I try using vibration with him. He is immediately so excited by this that he snatches the vibrating unit and it is hard work getting him to part with it. I should have had two in order to make it an Interactive Intervention.

Ryan is seven years old. He is more able than he appears and has a reasonable understanding of speech. He enjoys painting but spends much of his time striding around the room tapping the walls in specific places. In his case it appears that his knocking tells him where he is, rather than being a source of rhythmic stimulus. When I walk around with him he does notice and gives me brief eye contact. The best response from him is when he is standing looking through a glass door. I stand behind him with my hands firmly on his shoulders and tap his rhythm. Now he is interested.

The next two boys, Jaleel and Ahmad, are also completely withdrawn into worlds of their own. Jaleel is nine. He looks anxious and seems afraid of the other children, preferring to keep out of their way. He holds a toy: a drum with pegs that push in and out when it is wheeled. Most of the time he holds the toy up and taps the pegs with his fingers. Alternatively he plays with a hammer, tapping it against his head. When I tap the same rhythms on the table he sits down at the other end and gradually stretches out his hand to touch my arm and gently stroke it.

Ahmad is also nine. He is standing between the window and the table, flicking the surface in a pool of sunlight. At first I think that this is simply another tapping feedback game until he starts to make shadows on the wall. What he is really interested in is the visual feedback he is giving himself and he is delighted when I join in this game with him. I have to be careful not to make any sudden movements as these frighten him and he jumps but he always comes back for more. Ahmad makes sounds and prefers it when these are answered in a low pitch. He becomes very calm. Approaching my head, he touches my hand and briefly rests his forehead on mine.

# Samir and the kazoo

Finally I am introduced to Samir who is seven years old. I suspect that rather than straight autism it would be more accurate to describe his condition as a pervasive learning disability with possible autistic features. He has no speech and his responses do involve a delay. He is small for his age, floppy and has a large head. He cannot walk although he has recently learned to pull himself up and stagger around a table.

Samir wants to get out of the room. He sits by the door crying. I answer his sad sounds with empathetic ones of my own, playing around with the ones he is making. I feel he is not as responsive as I would have expected so instead of using my voice, I start to respond with a kazoo to enhance my responses. He begins to pay more attention to my answers, realising that they are contingent to his. Each time I make a sound he thinks about it and then after a few seconds interval wraps me in his enormous grin. He looks carefully, eventually imitating my action, pursing his lips and trying to blow two or three times. When I lean over him from behind and touch my forehead to his, he leans back repeatedly for me to do it again. Eventually he pulls himself up on a table and crawls over it towards me saying, 'Bb-bb-bb' (Turkish for 'daddy').

One of the reasons that Samir is utterly enchanting is that his smile involves not only his mouth, but also his eyes. Somehow it manages to reach out and embrace his partner with its warmth. Another aspect of his ability to relate is due to the delay in his response. When I clap his hand he rolls on his back and looks at it. After a time he flexes his fingers carefully, one by one, first on one hand and then on the other. The next time I put out my hand he is able to bring his to mine, at first gently and the following time to pat my fingers. When he manages to do this, his responses suggest that he has already thought carefully about what I am doing, it just takes time for him to organise his physical response. So what he is thinking becomes visible to the observer. His brain recognises what I am doing and considers it, showing that he does so through his related physical actions. He needs to sense what he thinks in order to know what it is.

Reflecting on why Samir's responses are so attractive to me brings to mind that some of the most profound verbal conversations in which I have ever been involved, ones I have been most deeply drawn into, have been with a conversation partner whose replies are not instantaneous but who takes a brief interval to reflect on what I have said before answering. Somehow this pause pays tribute to my offering (validating it as worth reflecting on). While Samir's delayed response appears to be due to the difficulty he has in linking up his perception with organising his motor response, the effect is the same. However difficult, he has taken the trouble to consider what I have initiated and his response is joyful. What else can one ask in terms of relationship?

# What does the behaviour tell us?

What is the point of these intimate encounters, these delightful conversations?

All of the adults and children we have met are locked into a deeply distressing and often painful sensory world. They are unable to relate to people in any way. While we may occasionally be able to train them, we cannot teach them unless we have their attention.

We cannot do this while they are beating their heads on the wall or swallowed in a repetitive maze. Before we can begin to think about slotting them into our educational curricula it is absolutely imperative that we find ways of getting in touch with them, relating to their sensory distress rather than, as so often at present, their behaviour. We must find ways of introducing them to the possibilities of emotional engagement, to the potential for joy in being human.

Contacting the school about two months after the visit, I enquired whether the interventions were continuing and if so what effect they were having. The answer was almost casual: 'Oh, Intensive Interaction, that's something we use all the time now, in fact we have been showing another school.'

Pursuing a curriculum through an inappropriate communication system is like trying to email someone who is still using smoke signals. It is not that our partner does not want to communicate – witness the smiles on their faces as soon as the brain picks up signals it recognises. Every time we try to interact we have to ask: 'Does what I am doing have meaning for my partner?' The more we are prepared to explore their body language, the more we can learn about their sensory sensitivities and which of our activities help or do not help to reduce the pain and anxiety this triggers, thus freeing up their brain to operate more effectively.

# Chapter 10

# Behind the

## Recognition

Recognition of self is not just a human attribute. Elephants, dolphins and now it appears, even magpies see themselves in the mirror, not just as any old magpie, elephant or dolphin but as 'individual me' magpies etc. Marking a magpie's throat with black dots where it cannot normally see them and placing the bird in front of a mirror leads it to attempt to dislodge them. The magpie recognises its own image and knows that it is distorted, not as it should be.[132] Such intellectual prowess is unexpected in a bird with a brain roughly the size of a pea and probably evolved separately from mammalian self-recognition. The question is what light, if any, does such avian prowess shed on human self-consciousness? Simply knowing our dimensions (in the broadest sense), is not the same as feeling that the image I see is necessarily 'me'. So what do I mean by 'me'?

## Panning for self

Looking for self is like panning for a reflection trapped between the twin mirrors of affect and cognition. The more I search, the more elusive the ultimate image is, and yet the eye continues to be drawn further and further inward in pursuit of this mysterious entity called I. What is 'I' and where does I begin and 'not I' start? What is the relationship between self, image, identity and reflection?

---

132 Prior H , Schwarz A & Güntürkün O (2008) Mirror-induced behaviour in the magpie (*Pica pica*): evidence of self-recognition. *PLoS Biology* **August 2008**.

...sical question of what we mean by a feeling of self is ...always teased philosophers (and now psychologists ...biologists) as it involves consideration of what we mean ...iousness. If we take the Descartian adage, 'I think therefore ...and its first cousin, 'I am therefore I think', they present us ...vastly oversimplified pictures of unadulterated perception ...reaming from a monolithic self. In fact it is clear that both what we 'feel' and what we 'think' are the outcome of a struggle between literally millions of stimuli battling for priority, versus all of our memories and defences.

# Imitation games

Vast swathes of research in developmental psychology are now devoted to the imitation games played by mother and infant, partly in the hope of unlocking the mystery of exactly when an infant becomes conscious of itself – an event that recent research indicates is being pushed back closer and closer to the actual birth. If an infant can copy its mother's mouth movements at 20 minutes old, then it is already establishing in its brain that the sensory patterns it receives from the external world are equivalent to the motor patterns it feels inside itself. It seems likely that the advent of consciousness of self is a gradual process rather than a blinding flash, and still continues to reach into adulthood when we become conscious of odd corners that have so far evaded our notice. Rather than being located in a specific area of the brain, it is now suggested that conciousness is more in the nature of a conversation between different areas of the brain [133]. However, as Raymond Tallis points out, consciousness is a one-way ticket. Except for catastrophic damage there is no way back.[134]

In practice, any description of the mother-infant dyadic interactions as copying, mimicking or imitation is misleading, since they clearly consist of far more than direct mimicry. Both mother and baby use them to enlarge rather than contain the boundaries of the arena in which they are played.

---

133 Simon van Gaal, Neurospin Institute Paris. Reported in: Peck ME (2011) Signal for consciousness in brain marked by neural dialogue. *Scientific American Mind* **November/December**.
134 Tallis R (2008) *The Kingdom of Infinite Space*. London: Atlantic Books.

To address the question of what it is that imitation does for us and why it is so riveting, we need to think of it in sensory terms. I am an infant. When I wave my arms, I receive sensory feedback and feel the movement in myself as I do it: my body tells my brain that I am doing it. But now, when my mother waves her arm back to me, or repeats my sound, I get visual (or auditory) feedback from outside of myself as well as information about my senses. I see and recognise my movement out there, or hear the sound that matches the one I felt as well as heard myself making. Not only is this confirmation and reinforcement of my neuronal pathways but my attention is drawn to a world out there beyond my immediate sensations – and one that I can to some extent control. I can relate to it and I begin to build up a picture of myself in context.

# Introduction to the mirror

With or without mother, such games are enormously enhanced when they are played in the presence of a mirror. Each time I make an initiative my inward sensory perception is confirmed from outside by a response in an alternative sense. One can think of it as triangulation of different modes of sensory experience, all pointing to the same thing, my awakening sense of me. In my expanding world, I gurgle with joy.

# Suspicion of the mirror

As I grow, my relationship with the mirror becomes more sophisticated. The child who stands in front of the mirror and decides that she would like to be wearing a pink dress with blue ribbons and yellow buttons is using it to test out variations on the theme of a self that is already clearly established. (Fortunately tastes change.) But an element of doubt remains: 'That mirror – I'm not quite sure that it's not deceiving me on the sly, just pretending to reflect my actions.' An anthropomorphic question mark dangles over its specious face. Does 'it' have an independent role in our exchanges?

So we move into investigative mode, one that is portrayed so vividly in the mirror scene in the film *Duck Soup*.[135] Ignorant of the Marx Brothers' elaboration, the child stands in front of the mirror and watches her reflection with deep attention. If she flicks her hand very quickly – there – maybe she can outrun her image. When this experimental approach fails she does not abandon her investigation, but in the best scientific tradition, tries an alternative approach. Turning her head away, she looks back out of the corner of her eye, hoping to catch the mirror doing something different while it thinks she is not looking. No luck. Disappointed by this teasing discrepancy between expectation and outcome she walks round the back to make sure she's not there; she is accompanied by a cat. What do they hope to find?

Big disappointment: there is nothing. Scratch the silver coating on the back and a streak of light reveals the see-through nature of glass.

# Strategies of projection

Having decided that our image does indeed reflect ourselves, we go on to use it for both recognition and reassurance. On a surface level, we look in the mirror to see if we are tidy, to pat our hair or to bolster our courage before going out to meet someone. A slightly less passive role is suggested by some rather curious experiments indicating that we behave better when we are in the presence of a mirror. In this research, students exhibited significantly less racial prejudice when a mirror was present in the room. The researchers concluded that this was because mirrors make us more aware of ourselves.[136]

Mukhopadhyay looks in the mirror and sees colours which tell him stories. When he writes about this it seems that he is identifying and objectifying processes in his brain in the mirror, he is watching his thinking in the mirror.[137]

---

135 *Duck Soup* (1933) Film. Directed by Leo McCarey. Pasadena, CA: Paramount Pictures.
136 Wickens C & Stapel D (2008) The mirror and I: when private opinions are in conflict with public norms. *Journal of Experimental Social Psychology* **44** (4) 1160–1166.
137 Mukhopadhyay TR (2008) *How Can I Talk if My Lips Don't Move? Inside my autistic mind.* New York: Arcade Publishing.

But for all of us there is an element of doubt. Like Alice, maybe, just maybe, we can persuade the looking glass to melt and take us a little further into ourselves, however frightening an experience this turns out to be. As we know, such adventures into our interior can be truly terrifying.

This looking-glass identity is precarious. Taken as a young child on a quick trip around Madame Tussauds I bolted for the door, shocked not so much by waxworks of famous murderers and instruments of torture but by an introduction to distorting mirrors. As my carefully constructed features wobbled and took off in a way that no longer supported self-image, they were anything but funny. Having already established for my own satisfaction that light travels in straight lines, something had gone badly wrong. Rather than doubt the physical properties of silver-backed glass I assumed the deviation was in myself. It was many years before I was prepared to enter into dialogue with distortion.

However, over and above its physical properties, the mirror can and does reflect our aliveness and feeling of self, to the extent that we may feel that our image is our self. Sometimes, in the case of people with autism, this image may be perceived as the self that is known to exist but which cannnot be sensed physically.

I am walking through a gallery in Tate St Ives. On the wall is a line drawing by Ben Nicholson of a woman peering into a mirror. As we see her, her head is side view but is so placed that the image that peers back reflects the full-view face. Close attention reveals a discrepancy between the subject and her image: where her face looking into the mirror has no features, no eyes, no lips, no nostrils, the image that looks out with penetrating gaze is so clearly defined that, although the notes do not tell us who the subject is, it is clearly recognisable as Nicholson's wife, Barbara Hepworth. This is confirmed by a letter that Nicholson wrote to a friend in 1966:

> 'Yes, I always liked the drawing of Barbara looking in the mirror, it was a strange ornate white framed oval mirror ... I have always liked the idea of the reflection being more actual than the object reflected.'[138]

---
138 Nicholson B (1966) Letter from Ben Nicholson to Nicolette Grayson, 14th January.

So where am I? If I am having problems with knowing who I am, (and splitting off the bits I don't like, or which I am told are 'bad') there is a temptation to project my expectations, fantasies and despair on the mirror's passive and unforgiving surface and think that this is where my real self resides.

The tendencies towards projection and introjection are strategies available to us all, whether or not we are on the autistic spectrum. For example, Pippa, a three-year-old child who is not autistic, is temporarily being looked after by a woman whose previous charge, Enid, has died. In her grief she persistently talks about Enid, making what seem to be unfavourable comparisons. Pippa wakes one day to the notion that to be loved she must be Enid and from now on she sees herself as this dead but living child, refusing to answer to any other name. Eventually she is 'rescued' from this aberrant situation by her returning mother, who points out that she is not Enid, but the Pippa whom she loves. However, withdrawal from her projection is accompanied by a feeling of loss and of having been in another place.

# Different voices

This particular difficulty is highlighted by the behavioural strategies adopted by some verbal or at least semi-verbal people on the autistic spectrum. In order to explore this I shall (as I have already done in *From Isolation to Intimacy*[139]) draw on Donna Williams' extraordinarily revealing exploration of her loss of feeling of self and her consequent relationship with mirrors. I do this because, having now a very wide experience of working with many different adults and children on the autistic spectrum, I want to draw attention to the particular predicament she describes, one that I believe is being largely overlooked. It manifests in two different ways, which seem to me to be interconnected. The first is that the individual uses two or more quite distinct voices to cover different ways of relating to those they meet. Their 'bad voice' – the one that expresses how they feel (and is rejected by us as being socially unacceptable), and the other – their 'good voice', reflecting what they have been taught they ought to feel.

---

139 Caldwell P & Horwood J (2007) *From Isolation to Intimacy: Making friends without words*. London: Jessica Kingsley Publishers.

Having lost touch with how they really feel, the second characteristic, (which is sometimes but not always present), links in to their sense of self, or rather its absence, in that a number of these individuals are fascinated by mirrors. Asked which of them recognised this combination at a meeting of 30 parents with children on the autistic spectrum, at least half put up their hands.

# Knowing where we are: the egocentric space

Two factors seem to be underlying this loss of self. The first arises from a failure to recognise sensory boundaries, to have no picture of physical self and where self stops and other begins. On a personal note, I (who do not have autism), know where I am as a result of feedback from my tactile and proprioceptive organs: the sensors in my skin define my shape. I feel my feet on the floor, the seat of the chair and the pressure of the mattress. The wind on my skin tells me the shape of my face. We live at the centre of an egocentric space, which as Raymond Tallis points out, is not the same as the physical space that we inhabit, since we prioritise those parts of our environment, or objects in it, which are of special interest.[140] 'My world' is that to which I give attention or that which forces its attention on me. As I write, I am waiting to open the door to a friend. Not having secured the latch, a gentle wind blows it open but no one comes in – slightly spooky. Both unexpected absence and anticipated presence have my attention. At other times the door is not on my priority list so it is not something I take notice of. Even when I am sitting at my desk in close proximity, I ignore it.

To quote Raymond Tallis:

> 'The sense of I is lost in and wakes out of, the world in which it engages ... the experiences that make our experiences of our bodies all add up to the moment of "I" consciousness. There is a unity of apperception ... that we may think of as the convergence point of our

---

140 Tallis R (2008) *The Kingdom of Infinite Space.* London: Atlantic Books.

*attention ... the location of the attending self – the centre of the egocentric space.'*[141]

So far, locating my 'self' is easy; but what if my interpretation of incoming signals is that they are weak or overwhelming or distorted in some other way? What picture do I get of myself then? What is my experience of myself if I am hyposensitive to touch and don't feel my outline, or I cannot understand the way that I am both connected to and separated from my physical environment?

# Lost selves

To begin with there are the physical consequences. Donna Williams describes how, in order to process at least some of her sensory intake, her sense of seeing or of feeling would shut down. At any one time she could either see or feel but not both at the same time. As a consequence she flapped her hand, in the mistaken belief that it was just an irritating object floating in front of her, so she tried to get rid of it. She either saw it (but could not feel that it was attached) or felt it (but could not see it as part of herself).[142]

In this instance, which she describes as taking place over two years, Williams does not seem to have the physical map (that we all take for granted) of where she stops and 'other' starts. One of the consequences of this is that 'out there' can be extremely invasive since it has a habit of suddenly popping up 'inside' without warning. No boundaries means no territorial defences, which can be very threatening.

However, the need to feel embodied extends beyond the physical into the less well-defined domain of the psyche. The terminology shifts from 'feeling earthed' and 'having our feet on the ground' to 'being centred' (as opposed to, 'feeling all over the place'). Where we look for our un-centred or 'lost' selves depends in which sense we are talking about self and where we perceive that self ought to be. When we say that our sense of self is lost, is more missing than just our physical awareness of sensory feedback from out there?

---

141 Tallis R (2008) *The Kingdom of Infinite Space.* London: Atlantic Books.
142 Williams D (1996) *Autism: An inside out approach: An innovative look at the mechanics of autism and its developmental cousins.* London: Jessica Kingsley Publishers.

Listen to Williams again as she describes how she looked for herself in the mirror, convinced that she was in the image that she saw reflected, to the extent that for two years she tried to walk through the mirror in order to reach what she saw as her self.[143] Now we are looking at affective perception rather than physical image. It is not that she does not know *that* she exists, but rather that because of her low level of sensory intakes, she has mislaid her perception of *where* she exists.

This is not surprising, given that in her remarkable description of her early life Williams describes herself as having three different characters, each with a different voice.[144] She would move from one to another in order to relate to the particular situation in which she found herself at the time. One can think of these as free-floating adaptations, allowing her to pass herself off – just as Pippa used Enid – in situations that would otherwise be intolerable. People use these adaptations not just to hide from the world outside but also as a shield to protect themselves from their own vulnerability and pain, (and in the case of autism, from the overwhelming demands placed on an overloaded processing system and our reactions to their subsequent behaviour).

Exactly how this divorce between 'good voice' and 'bad voice' manifests itself varies from, on the one hand, secret phrases only uttered when the person is on their own, to the other end of the scale where the different voices speak to each other through puppets, ones that the individual has deliberately carved to serve the purpose. Between these two extremes there is a whole range of strategies but what they all have in common is the actualisation of a defensive system, particularly the bright cheerful voice that the person has learned is acceptable to the outside world. It is characteristic of this voice that although it may be saying all the right things, it often sounds unattached, almost that of an automaton: 'This is what I have been taught to say in order for you to accept me.' This tonal rift is the result of our rejection of the person's negative feelings – 'You mustn't say that, it is naughty/nasty' – since we cannot bear their pain and feel as though it is personally directed against us.

---

143 Williams D (1996) *Autism: An inside out approach: An innovative look at the mechanics of autism and its developmental cousins.* London: Jessica Kingsley Publishers.
144 Williams D (1998) *Nobody Nowehere: The remarkable authoboigraphy of an autistic girl.* London: Jessica Kingsley Publishers.

Chapter 10: Behind the mirror

I have already explored three of the following stories in the context of 'learned voices' [145]. This time I want to think about them to see what light they may throw on what we mean when we talk about 'I'.

Lizzy expresses how she feels through completely different voices, one cheerful and one (sometimes) savage as she struggles to come to terms with the negative responses she receives and images she has of herself. Contrast the welcoming, 'Hello, Phoebe, how are you?' alongside a deep growling, 'I want to hit Phoebe, I want to hit her', said almost in the same breath. The former articulates a learned attitude, what she has been told she ought to say, and the latter expresses her suppressed feeling. When I acknowledge this darkness: 'You must feel like hitting Phoebe?' there is a third voice, centred and breathing relief. 'Oh, yes I do.' Someone has understood how she really feels and acknowledged this. Since our sense of who we are is largely derived from what we feel ourselves to be, acknowledging her negative self allows Lizzy to be who she really feels she is, a position from which she is normally divorced since she is barred from feeling and expressing her 'bad bits'.

Jim has several different voices including a telephone answering voice that he has clearly picked up from his mother, one for when he is surprised and another he uses with his support staff. However, every day he stays for some time in his room shouting abuse at his image in the mirror. His bad self has taken temporary lodgings in his reflection.

Mike, who used to talk to his mother but has given this up, has a 'good hand' and a 'bad hand', who talk to each other. At school he is subject to a behavioural programme that requires him to sit on the naughty chair if he is seen to be misbehaving. As this programme takes a grip he comes to see himself as naughtier and naughtier. Mike's good hand disappears and his bad hand takes over: he uses it to self-injure, hitting his head and screaming. Nothing will console him. Trying to talk back his good hand is a failure; it is like trying to relate to a mirror image – there is nothing there that can respond. What is successful when he is upset, is using his non-verbal sounds to empathise with him. When his brain hears these answers to his despair Mike quietens down to listen almost

[145] Caldwell P & Horwood J (2007) *From Isolation to Intimacy: Making friends without words*. London: Jessica Kingsley Publishers.

immediately. Now if he is upset he even enlists his mother's aid, saying, 'Mum, bad hand is bullying me again.'

A different story is told by the Dave who talks to himself quietly when he is sitting in his room about where he is going and in which vehicle he will be travelling. 'I'll go in the red car/the green lorry.' He only uses this, his relaxed speech, when he thinks no one is listening. It is his secret conversation with himself. Dave's public speech is in his angry voice, which surfaces and lets rip when he is becoming upset. (It clearly derives from his experience in a long-stay hospital for – as it was then known – people with mental handicap.) In situations he finds stressful Dave spins round shouting, 'I'll get sister, I'll get sister', becoming increasingly loud as his agitation increases; he ends up hitting anyone who is near. When he is upset, this cycle can be broken by placing his two voices alongside each other, saying, 'You'll have to get sister in a green car.' The surprise of this unexpected juxtaposition jolts his brain sufficiently to attract his attention away from his inner turmoil and stops him in his tracks.

Looking again at Pippa, who feels herself becoming Enid, once the split is made, exactly where the sense of self-awareness ends up seems to depend on the particular need that it fulfils. For Pippa there is no sitting on the fence. She is looking for an absent love so she gives herself totally to becoming Enid, even if in retrospect she is aware of the displacement from one person to the other. In other respects, she is unaware of the displacement, this is who and where she is. It is only outsiders who are puzzled by her insistence on being called Enid. As far as she is concerned, this is her name.

Donna's situation is much more complicated. Mistreated as a child, and under siege from a world that is impossible to interpret, she adopts her alter egos as defence mechanisms against circumstances that she finds intolerable. Where Pippa is 'running to', Donna is hiding herself from others and in the process losing her sense of where she is. But not entirely. Unlike Pippa, she is at least aware that something is missing. She goes looking for herself in the mirror – in the dimensions and form that she recognises as herself but does not feel herself to be.

Lizzy is also defensive and can be aggressive when upset. Like Donna, she 'manages to relate' by using language that she has learned is publicly acceptable, but in doing so she is camouflaging a whole pile of distress that erupts when she feels threatened. She is also fascinated by her image in the mirror, as are a number of people with good voices and bad voices. It is only when her distress is acknowledged that we hear her real self, a completely different and centred presentation, relaxed, humorous and charming.

Jim has taken on board the abuse he has received in the past and projected it into his mirror. When he is relaxed he talks sadly but calmly about the family, home and children he so desires but does not have.

Mike does not want to be bad but the behavioural programme to which he is subject continually reinforces his negative side, to the point where it is all he has. Stripped of any sense of his goodness he attacks himself. Redemption, if one can call it this, is not through building up his split-off (phantom) good self but by appealing to the person he really is, addressing his inner self through body language uncontaminated by his projection.

Dave is vulnerable in a different way. Oversensitive to his internal feedback, he is embarrassed if people hear him talking to himself about the subject that interests him – where he is going and how – and he hides this need to know what he is doing. He only really interacts with the outside world when he is overcome by other people's raised voices.

# Battling on two fronts

The problem for people on the autistic spectrum is that they are battling on two fronts, not only with their sensory disorder but also with our rejection of the behaviours triggered by this internal chaos. In fact we all use different voices, moderating or sharpening our tone according to whether we are calm or disturbed. However, in the situations I have described, the individual is not merely dipping in and out of protective strategies but is becoming trapped in their alternative self. Rather than ignoring this situation we need to look at the vulnerability that it indicates and ask ourselves what the pressures are that are stressing our partners so much that they become displaced, dislocated in a way that compounds their autism. This may be a way of retreating that is more subtle than shutting one's eyes, turning one's back or simply cutting out awareness of people, but it is equally effective in separating us from each other.

## The self on watch

One of the things that we learn from people with autism is that they may be deeply aware when they are becoming confused; even then there is part of their brain that can and does monitor the slippage. Remember the child with autism who says his brain is running away and another who likens her brain to tangled spaghetti (Chapter 2)? Both are observing their cognitive capacity slip round the corner to the point where it no longer functions in any sense that is useful to them. But there is still a part of them that observes this happening. Importantly, when the capacity for rational processing and thought are obscured, it is still possible to make connection through sensation and affect if we use signals that are part of the brain's normal repertoire. Even if our partner is self-injuring, we can offer them safe harbour from the autonomic storm by using their rhythms and sounds, particularly if these include slight deviations. This is the affective anchor, 'the delicious conversation' that, when the cognitive processing is disappearing, 'feels like being thrown a life-belt in a stormy sea when one is drowning'.[146] Confirmation is at the centre of this rescue bid. It offers an escape route, switching focus from the closed inner brain-body conversation to the world outside, physically embedding the sense of self within relationship. Confirmation can even be used to anticipate a particular behaviour, stopping it before it has started by shifting attention before the brain has a chance to lock into the inner world, as in the following story.

Mike comes out of the bathroom saying anxiously, 'My teeth are white' and hits the nearest person unless this is confirmed. But, if one can get in first when the bathroom door opens, saying, 'Your teeth are white', Mike laughs and shows no sign of aggression.

---

146 Williams D (1995) *Jam Jar*. Film. Fresh Film in association with Channel 4, UK.

# A different mirror

In using body language with our autistic partners we are offering a different sort of mirror, one that reflects and responds and confirms them in a lively and demanding way, yet which is still restrained and respectful. One that rather than showing us what we look like, engages with us and when we reach intimacy allows us to see ourselves as others do. The feedback this image gives us will no longer be optical: we shall say that we 'feel moved' and our communication will be affective rather than cognitive.

So where has our sense of self gone? Does it resemble the atom, which we used to think of as the ultimate unit but now understand as a universe in itself of balancing forces with odd names such as 'quarks' and lending weight to any calculations, 'Higgs boson'? I suspect the self is more likely to be retrieved from the entity that decides whether or not to undertake the search, rather than in the bottomless pits of introspection. It is within the experience of intimacy that we find ourselves most closely defined.

# Chapter 11

# Joined up islands

## What do my partners feel?

For me, one of the reasons why Joshua's description of how it feels to be at the receiving end of Intensive Interaction is so appealing is that most of the people who I am involved with are non-verbal. My partners cannot tell me how they feel about our interactions except by their responsive behaviour as expressed through body language. This is important since I want to be quite sure that we are genuinely sharing our experience of each other, rather than me projecting my feelings onto them. Do they really feel the reality of exchange, the wonder and synchrony, or is it just that I feel good and imagine that my partner does too? And if we feel good about each other, and are learning about each other, what is happening to us in terms of the chemistry of affect?

## The sorting depot

One way of thinking about the brain is to visualise an intricate sorting depot. Information from the senses is separated into that which requires instant attention and less urgent messages which are forwarded more slowly, a kind of first class and second class mailing system. For example, dangerous situations, or even potentially dangerous ones may require an instant response, there is no time to hang around thinking about what to do, although that may come later. If we see a dangerous snake we fire off the body's self-defence processes. Without stopping to think what we are doing we run, freeze or hit it with a stick if there is one handy. We have mobilised the so-called fight or flight system.

# The delivery system: hormones and neurotransmitters

We have two ways of delivering messages from the brain around the body. The first is by fast-track neurotransmission. Messages carried along the long arms of the nerves by electrical impulses are shuttled across the small gap between one nerve and the next by chemicals known as neurotransmitters to specific places in the body. (Vivienne Parry suggests the helpful image of passing the baton between one nerve and the next.[147]) The second way of transferring the brain's instructions is through hormones, chemicals that originate in endocrine glands (glands that secrete the hormones in different parts of the body) and hitch a ride round the body in the bloodstream. These hormones only dock at the correct address if they encounter target cells that have matching built-in receptors: in mechanical terms, a lock and key system. In order to take effect, they have to find the right fit.

We have many different hormones carrying diverse messages, affecting everything from growth and sexual activity to regulation of our metabolism. In this rapidly expanding field there are now known to be hundreds. They tell our body what to do and are indirectly responsible for how we feel.

# Oxytocin and vasopressin

At present, while it is clear that there is a lot still to learn, there is much interest among researchers in neurochemistry about the role played by oxytocin (the so-called 'cuddle hormone' or 'love hormone') in promoting social attachment as we get to know each other.

The stress hormones (adrenalin and its longer term partner, cortisol) and their reactions have been extensively studied. Less well charted is exactly which hormones and neurotransmitters are active (and at what levels) in any particular calming or pleasurable experience. But it is clear that 'feeling good' is accompanied by increased levels of dopamine, serotonin and noradrenaline/

---

[147] Parry V (2005) *The Truth about Hormones*. London: Atlantic Books.

norepinephrine (along with other chemicals), and that this rise is mediated by oxytocin and its close relative vasopressin.[148]

## The effects of oxytocin

Among its many effects, oxytocin plays a major part in the recognisable cocktail that predicates engaging with or even seeing pictures of babies – the 'aaah' factor that women may experience when looking at the young. (I am amused to find this sensation rising through my body when watching an item on the TV news. An, aesthetically speaking, extremely ugly baby white rhino nuzzles its mother's teat – and off I go again.) Ratey suggests that the effect of such images is due to 'a small squirt of dopamine, serotonin and oxytocin into the pleasure centres'.[149] Every time we experience orgasm and every time we breastfeed our babies we are in the affective arms of oxytocin.

## The red-alert brain

However, to designate oxytocin as a 'feel-good hormone' is perhaps misleading, since its benefits appear to be backhanded, part of a system of checks and balances. Its function is to mediate a reduction of anxiety rather than being directly responsible for a so-called 'high'. Looked at this way, a somewhat negative picture emerges of a brain designed to be constantly on the alert and ready to assume the fight or flight course of action. To complicate matters, the brain's default position may be anywhere on the sliding scale of attentiveness, from overreaction (too much cortisol) to passive failure to react.

Kerstin Uvnäs-Moberg suggests that such a pessimistic view is due to researchers having focused on visible goal oriented activity – we focus on what we can see – whereas a system of calm and connectedness, while physiologically just as valuable in terms of body healing and growth, is invisible.[150] (From our point of view nothing is actually happening, in the sense that although we may feel its

---
148 Ratey J (2003) *A User's Guide to the Brain*. London: Abacus.
149 *Ibid*.
150 Uvnäs-Moberg K (2003) *The Oxytocin Factor: Tapping the hormone of calm, love and healing*. Cambridge, MA: Da Capo Press.

effects, we do not see its activity.) She points out that to function well we need to have a balance between exertion (and stress reaction) and calm. In terms of hormonal and neurotransmitter instigators, she contrasts the 'power drink' of the fight or flight reaction as opposed to the 'healing nectar' of calm and connectedness.

Although it is relatively small, like many organic molecules the structure of oxytocin is complex, consisting of nine amino acids linked in a circle with a tail – tadpole shaped. In structural terms, while it differs only slightly from vasopressin, the two operate in what appear to be opposing ways, one offsetting and damping down the other. While oxytocin is linked with calm, vasopressin is an instigator in the fight or flight response to stress. And oxytocin is not just a chemical present in humans: in evolutionary terms, it has been around a long time – it is even present in earthworms, where it appears to facilitate egg laying.[151] This is a function not so dissimilar to that which was first demonstrated in humans when oxytocin was discovered in 1906, where it was shown to be associated with contractions in the smooth muscle of the uterus, which expel the infant from the womb. From lowly invertebrate to vertebrate mammal, is it possible that expulsion of the young can still be mediated by the same process? Perhaps one should not be surprised if this is so, given its primary position in the struggle for survival. Why discard a system that works?

# A wider understanding of the functions of oxytocin

Further investigations established the activity of oxytocin in the process of breastfeeding, where contractions in the smooth muscle of the breast squeeze out the breast milk. At this stage oxytocin was thought of as a hormone present only in women during birth and nurturing but it is now known to be present in men as well. What has also become evident is that, apart from its links with reproduction, it is also involved in an astonishing spectrum of physiological and behavioural activities. These range from its effects on digestion, blood pressure and growth, to its ability to reduce anxiety and influence social interaction, to name but a few.

---

151 Uvnäs-Moberg K (2003) *The Oxytocin Factor: Tapping the hormone of calm, love and healing.* Cambridge, MA: Da Capo Press.

It now seems that one of the major roles of oxytocin is to link social contact with pleasure by mediating the release of dopamine (which feels good) and reducing the levels of anxiety associated with going out on a limb, putting oneself in the hands of another person. However indirectly, oxytocin improves our ability to trust others. Using a game that involved lending money to strangers, Paul Zac found that we are considerably more generous in offering money to people we don't know following injections of oxytocin.[152]

## Oxytocin and autism

Further research has led to the suggestion that, since one of the difficulties experienced by people on the autistic spectrum is that they have difficulties in relating to people, they may have a deficit in oxytocin receptors, so are unable to make the link between socialisation and pleasure. In some extremely interesting investigations, Hollander found that if autistic adults are given an intravenous oxytocin infusion it improves their ability to recognise emotions in people's voices.[153] Furthermore, while previous work had shown that when people on the autistic spectrum see faces it activates a part of the brain that would normally be used for object recognition, infusions of oxytocin restore normal processing so that facial recognition is improved. Additionally, repetitive behaviours are reduced by infusions of oxytocin. Put simplistically, giving a person with autism extra oxytocin makes it easier for them to relate, so presumably the converse is also true: that their difficulties in relating must be due to a deficit of this hormone.

## The joyful response to meaningful language

However, it is difficult to reconcile this idea with the sometimes overwhelming joy displayed when relationships are established

---

152 Kosfeld M, Heinrichs M, Zac P, Fischbacher U & Fehr E (2005) Oxytocin increases trust in humans. *Nature* **435** 673–676.

153 Hollander E, Bartz J, Chaplin W, Phillips A, Sumner J, Soorya L, Anagnostou E & Wasserman S (2006) Oxytocin increases retension of social cognition in autism. *Biological Psychiatry* **61** (4) 498–503.

during interactions with our severely autistic partners using their particular body language. If the problem is too few oxytocin receptors, how do they manage this?

The following is a summary of behavioural changes during a two-day intervention in a school. I was working with seven non-verbal severely autistic children over two mornings, (from whom staff were unable to elicit any meaningful responses). At first these boys and girls seemed completely switched off, interested only in their particular repetitive behaviours. After less than half an hour of using their body language with each child (separately) – and in some cases within a few minutes – six were smiling, four had extended their hands to touch my hand or arm (or in one case, the teacher's hand), two had shyly kissed my forehead and four were copying my behaviour and initiating 'games' based on elements of the common language we had developed. With the exception of one child who was particularly anxious, the children had moved from separation to friendly relationship. Even the affective state of the boy who was most disturbed had calmed. He was more attentive, causing the boy's support worker to volunteer that he could now see ways of interacting with him that he was anxious to try out, whereas previously it had been difficult to find any avenue through which to reach him. The fact that these children clearly enjoyed relationship once their anxiety level was reduced, suggests that the problem lies at least partially in sensory overload and fear of fragmentation, rather than in receptor deficit as such.

## A balance between anxiety and calm

Perhaps it is helpful to think of this paradox in terms of balance: the balance between anxiety and calm. On the one hand, people are experiencing high levels of anxiety due to a failure to process external and internal stimuli, and fear of overload and consequent autonomic storms. Once their stress levels are reduced by using their body language, even if people on the spectrum do have fewer oxytocin receptors, their brains would need less oxytocin to instigate a feeling of calm. Provided the incoming stimuli do not place a strain on the processing systems, then the weakened oxytocin system can cope. In behavioural terms, this is what happens.

If the neurochemistry of oxytocin is complex, so too are the subtleties of sensory experience now associated with it, scattered as they are through 'communing with nature', 'being in the zone', 'flow', fixation, friendship, sex, nurturing, love, and the heights of meditative experience. These affective or supra-affective states, while differing in the direction of the attentional searchlight, have in common the possibility of transcending self.

In behavioural terms, neurochemistry is telling us what we already know. 'No man is an island, entire of itself'[154] is the arch-truism: independence is an illusion, and our ability to relate is essential from the time we arrive struggling and kicking from our mother's womb. Even if as adults we prefer our own company, we are dependent on vast networks of people all over the world who make the materials for our clothes, provide warmth and heat, water and food and generally service our needs. Over and above all this, in the imperative for safety we search for acceptance from our peers and without it feel anxious and unsafe. Deprived of relationships we may turn our backs on the world or take on bravado – but it is a hollow bulwark. (The true hermit is an exception, in that they would not regard themselves as having withdrawn from the world but rather as having disengaged from its practicalities in order to engage more deeply with it through meditative practices.) It is not surprising that the brain is tuned in to helping companionship feel good.

# Changes in behaviour

Few of our autistic partners have the eloquence of Joshua and his 'delicious conversation'; the changes in our partner's ability and their desire to relate have to speak for their joy. While Joshua is telling us that body language conversations are a lifeline when he is overloaded and losing contact, a teaching assistant uses the same language to describe the connectedness that she feels by sharing a common and meaningful language with her students. She tells me

---

154 Donne J (1624) *Devotions upon Emergent Occasions and Seuerall Steps in my Sicknes: Meditation XVII.*

that working in a class with three very disturbed adolescent boys whom she has known for some years, she is afraid every day. She says she can never afford to turn her back, since she is still not sure what will happen if she takes her eyes off them. Such is her level of stress, that when she returns home at night the first thing she does is to pour herself a drink so that she can relax.

I introduce her to the idea of working through one of the student's own body language, demonstrating how to respond to all his sounds and movements. The next day I return to ask her how her interactions had gone. She laughs and says that it was the first night she had not reached for the bottle when she got home. She adds that at first when I talked about using body language to communicate, she thought I was a 'nutter' but when she tried it, it had changed how she could relate: 'It felt like having a conversation.' Like the small boy who linked the necklace he was stringing with the duplicate that his teacher was making (Chapter 5), we are joined up in a two-way process that takes us beyond just feeling good in ourselves to an intimate regard for our partner.

Much the same sentiments are expressed by three key workers who are supporting Brad, a young man who has recently left school, with a very negative reputation. He harms himself and others and smears faeces. The morning we meet he has already head-butted one of his key workers and tried to attack another. It is clear from his notes that he finds noises and large groups of people particularly difficult. I ask Mike (one of his key workers who is initially sceptical), to sit near Brad and use his body language to communicate with him.

To begin with I get Mike to return to Brad the split plastic cup he was playing with and which had been taken away. (When Brad feels its contours and listens to the crackly sound it makes, he knows what he is doing and can use these sensory inputs to focus on.) I suggest that Mike also plays with one in a similar fashion. Brad notices this and from facing away turns to sit facing Mike. They interact for some time with the cup, feeling it, sliding one piece against another and scraping it on the wall. Brad then drops the cup and moves on to stamping his feet and a variety of hand movements. Then he starts to copy Mike's hand movements including some quite complex ones such as sliding a pointed finger towards him on the sofa. This is particularly interesting since a number of current theories of autism are based on the supposed failure of people on the spectrum to copy hand movements, a finding which is out of line with the responses received when using a person's body language to communicate. Again and again, people with autism do copy what we do and extemporise on it, if we use signals that their brain recognises as familiar, which are already part of their repertoire. If they are really relaxed they can sometimes copy quite unfamiliar movements.

Brad moves to the swing and the interaction continues. The young man we see is cheerful, relaxed and attentive. It is not just his gestures that indicate his relaxation, but once he knows he will get answers to his non-verbal sounds (which had previously been minimal), they become more frequent and louder. In fun he pokes Mike and they laugh together. From a disturbed, switched off and distanced young man, Brad has changed into a cheerful and forthcoming partner. Here are the comments from his support staff to draw attention to how they felt about this transformation.

- 'I've never seen him like this before.'
- 'It feels empathetic.'
- '… real communication.'
- 'I feel emotional.'
- 'He just looks so happy.'
- 'This is not the Brad I know'.

Mike told me after Brad's lunch that they had continued using the approach throughout his meal and he had continued to enjoy it. In the afternoon training session Mike watched the DVD we had recorded during the morning's interventions and then, unprompted, said that while the film was alright and showed what had happened, he wanted to say (and here he struggled to express himself), that 'there was "more than" it showed'. It is this 'more than' quality, this over-and-above what physically happens, this affective flow, which so moves us.

We must also remind ourselves that we are talking about people with extreme autism. As partners paying each other intimate attention we move from one end of the relationship spectrum to the other: from the anxiety expressed in our reports as, 'Never turn your back because you may get hit' (and echoed in the person with autism by the fear of overloading stimuli), to trust and a desire to open ourselves out completely, to place ourselves totally in our partner's care. Curiosity and wonder mingle in shared exploration, beyond just feeling good about ourselves to being close to and caring for each other. This affective surge highlights the difference between 'feeling good' and 'intimacy'.

We can think of this dissimilarity as like playing ball, either by ourselves or with a friend. On our own we can be soothed by the rhythm of bouncing the ball repetitively against a wall – even if we throw it at different angles our response is tailored to our own initiative; our motor and reactive systems predict its return path and make allowances for any deviation. But when we play with a partner we place ourselves in their hands. The surprises they spring on us make the game more interesting, more fun. In order to keep up with them our sensory attention deepens until it is rooted in every movement they make, so firmly that there is an extent to which we become extensions of their play. Attending both externally to you and internally to myself, I feel the ebb and flow of what you feel. To speak of you 'becoming' in me is to crystallise such experience in my brain. At the same time as offering you what I am, I learn about the boundaries of myself. We feel joy in give-and-take exploration. We bathe in the running tide of each other.

Olly is restless. He wanders round his classroom, finding it difficult to settle or to relate. When he is upset he self-injures, hitting his head or chest. His breathing is noisy and sometimes he holds it. Since this is his focus, I tune into his breathing rhythm and he begins to take notice of me, coming to explore my face closely. I blow in his ear. He keeps on coming back. Eventually he stands with his back towards my front, reaches round and folds my hands across his chest. Every time he breathes I press on his chest. His face is ecstatic. Now he has a rhythm he recognises and can relate to but outside of himself. It makes sense. The next day I revisit his class and am sitting talking to his teacher. He comes and stands behind me and places his hands very gently either side of my head. He might have been giving a blessing.

On another occasion it is nearing the end of a day's workshop. A solid looking young man sitting near the back stops me in my tracks. 'It's all very well telling us about these techniques but what you're actually talking about is love, isn't it?' Ah, rumbled. But at the same time, 'yes' and 'no'. Perhaps it would be more accurate to say that in laying ourselves aside we adopt the strategies of love – attention, exploration, tenderness – and in doing so are drawn into intimacy, an intimacy that is unique to us.

One may question whether it is proper to initiate this depth of affect and then break away; can it be damaging to raise expectation and then leave? With my partners on the autistic spectrum, continuity and consistency are vital. Suspending interaction leads to regression. Nevertheless, once the capacity to relate is established it is normally easy to renew. One can think of this apparent contradiction as taking a step upwards and then back down, but the ability to know where one should put one's foot to regain the upper step remains. As in meiosis, where parts of the genome are exchanged and something new is created, what we generate in intimacy crystallises internally so there is no sense of loss afterwards. And we can all do it for each other. What we have is now part of us; we have fallen into each other's minds. Each time we add a particular flavour of well-being to our partner's and our own experience. This is what intimate attention to a partner offers both participants in the 'as-we-are-now' dyadic interaction.

# What do we feel?

In order to explore and fully engage with the world outside ourselves we should learn to use all of our different ways of appreciating its richness, not just through our sensory experience of its properties (and thinking about these) but also through affective appreciation, allowing ourselves to feel our responses to our environment and the people we meet. But bearing in mind that, in contrast to reasoning, affective reflection is broadcast rather than unidirectional, we also need to monitor our perceptions. They are best thought of as possibilities rather than certainties and as such, are probably not all going to be right. Nevertheless, they take us out of the straightjacket of personal experience and into the heart of delicious conversations.